Crafting and entertaining are two of my favorite pastimes.

Both of these creative efforts bring a feeling of closeness with my family and friends. Planning personalized parties with beautifully crafted decorations, plus a stunning table and accessories, turn our special occasions into memorable events.

I invite you to come entertain with us and be inspired to create easy, fast and elegant party pieces. *Spellbinders™ Quick & Easy Crafts for Entertaining* will share with you our projects, tips and techniques to easily personalize your next event using Spellbinders™ Paper Arts innovative craft tools. Our extensive line of products provides the versatility to cut, emboss and stencil a variety of materials for any occasion.

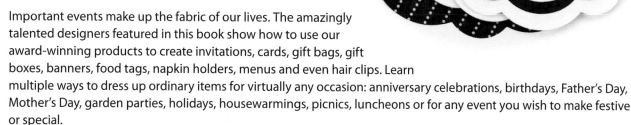

Important events make up the fabric of our lives. The amazingly talented designers featured in this book show how to use our award-winning products to create invitations, cards, gift bags, gift boxes, banners, food tags, napkin holders, menus and even hair clips. Learn multiple ways to dress up ordinary items for virtually any occasion: anniversary celebrations, birthdays, Father's Day, Mother's Day, garden parties, holidays, housewarmings, picnics, luncheons or for any event you wish to make festive or special.

I would like to thank all of the very gifted designers featured in *Spellbinders™ Quick & Easy Crafts for Entertaining*. Their creativity continues to amaze me, and I eagerly anticipate each and every project they design! They inspire me to continue with my passion of developing the very best crafting tools that provide spectacular design opportunities, value and versatility. I'd also like to thank all our supporters. They have made it possible for us to continue to produce the one-of-a-kind crafting tools Spellbinders™ is known worldwide for. And I want to extend a very special thank you to DRG for providing their publishing expertise, making it possible for us to share our inspiration for all of you to enjoy.

Happy entertaining,

Stacey Caron

Stacey Caron *is the creative force behind Spellbinders™ innovative designs and product lines. She has been scrapbooking and stamping for a number of years, and her enthusiasm for paper crafts truly inspires others. She has taught throughout the United States and internationally for retailers, private groups, scrapbook and stamping stores, distributors and sales rep groups. Prior to establishing Spellbinders, Stacey worked as a registered dental hygienist. She and her husband Jeff have been married for 17 years and have two sons, Nathan and Justin.*

Spellbinders™ Quick & Easy Crafts for Entertaining

EDITOR Tanya Fox

CREATIVE DIRECTOR Brad Snow

PUBLISHING SERVICES DIRECTOR
Brenda Gallmeyer

MANAGING EDITOR Brooke Smith

GRAPHIC DESIGNER Nick Pierce

COPY SUPERVISOR Deborah Morgan

COPY EDITORS Emily Carter, Mary O'Donnell

TECHNICAL EDITOR Corene Painter

PHOTOGRAPHY SUPERVISOR Tammy Christian

PHOTO STYLISTS Tammy Liechty,
Tammy Steiner

PHOTOGRAPHY Matthew Owen

PRODUCTION ARTIST SUPERVISOR
Erin Brandt

PRODUCTION ARTIST Nicole Gage

TECHNICAL ARTIST Debera Kuntz

PRODUCTION ASSISTANTS Marj Morgan,
Judy Neuenschwander

ISBN: 978-1-59635-390-9
Printed in USA
1 2 3 4 5 6 7 8 9

Spellbinders™ Quick & Easy Crafts for Entertaining is published by DRG, 306 East Parr Road, Berne, IN 46711. Printed in USA. Copyright © 2011 DRG. All rights reserved. This publication may not be reproduced in part or in whole without written permission from the publisher.

RETAIL STORES: If you would like to carry this pattern book or any other DRG publications, visit DRGwholesale.com.

Every effort has been made to ensure that the instructions in this publication are complete and accurate. We cannot, however, take responsibility for human error, typographical mistakes or variations in individual work. Please visit AnniesCustomerCare.com to check for pattern updates.

4 Special Techniques

Die Cutting

Cut shapes with Spellbinders™ die templates by creating a die-cutting sandwich.

1. Stack items in the following order: Base Plate; die template, cutting edge up; cardstock; and Cutting Plate (photo 1).

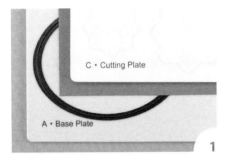

2. Keeping the sandwich flat and straight, insert it into the die-cutting/embossing machine. Turn the handle until the sandwich exits the other side of the machine (photo 2).

3. Remove the sandwich.

4. Open the sandwich to reveal the die cut (photo 3).

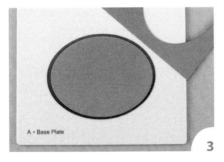

Tip: Save the die cut from the window for another project!

Embossing

To emboss die-cut shapes, create an embossing sandwich with the die-cut shape still placed within the die template.

1. Stack items in the following order: Base Plate; die template, cutting edge up with cardstock still in die template; Embossing Mat; and Embossing Plate (photo 4).

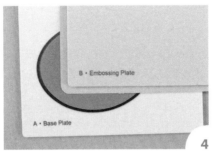

2. Keeping the sandwich flat and straight, insert it into the die-cutting/embossing machine. Turn the handle until the sandwich exits the other side of the machine.

3. Remove the sandwich.

4. Open the sandwich top to reveal the die-cut/embossed shape (photo 5).

Die Cutting & Embossing Stamped Images

Getting perfect placement to cut stamped images with Spellbinders™ die templates is so simple!

1. Stamp an image onto paper or cardstock.

2. Place die template over stamped image, cutting side down; center die for perfect placement (photo 6).

3. Use repositionable tape to secure die template onto paper or cardstock.

4. Run through die-cutting/embossing machine to cut (photo 7). Follow Embossing instructions to emboss this piece if desired.

Tip: Tape die template to paper on outer edge of die template to avoid damage to stamped image.

Making a Shaped Card

Why be limited to standard-shape cards when you can use Spellbinders™ die templates to make custom-shaped cards?

1. Form a top- or side-folded card.

2. Place folded edge of card inside die template cutting line (photo 8).

3. Use repositionable tape to secure die template to card.

4. Run through die-cutting/ embossing machine to create a custom-shaped and embossed card (photo 9).

Making Windows

Whether you want to make a window for a card front or a window in an altered book, the technique is the same. Spellbinders™ die templates make creating windows easy!

1. Use repositionable tape to secure die template to cardstock for perfect placement.

2. Run through die-cutting machine.

Tip: Save the die cut from the window for another project!

Making Frames

Create the perfect paper frame without the tedious work of using a craft knife. Spellbinders™ Nestabilities® die templates make the process super simple!

1. Choose two die templates in desired shapes.

2. Secure larger die template to cardstock with repositionable tape. This will be the outside edge of the frame.

3. Nest smaller die template inside larger die template; secure with repositionable tape. This will make the opening of the frame (photo 10).

4. Run through die-cutting machine to create a custom-shaped frame.

Tip: Don't limit yourself to one shape; mix and match die templates from different sets to create custom-shaped and sized frames. Save inside die cut to use on another project.

Selective Die Cutting

Stretch your creativity in die cutting! Try selective cutting to further customize your crafts.

1. Place cardstock over a portion of die template (photo 11).

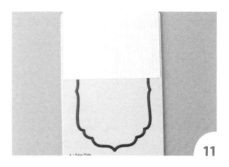

2. Secure in place with repositionable tape.

3. Run through die-cutting machine to create a custom die-cut image.

Tissue-Paper Carnation

What a quick and clever way to make tissue-paper carnations!

1. Fold a large sheet of tissue paper in half; continue folding until you have 12–16 layers of tissue paper.

2. Die-cut folded tissue paper using a circular die template such as Dahlia (photo 12).

3. Punch two small holes through center; thread floss or string through holes and tie a double knot; trim ends to ¼ inch (photo 13).

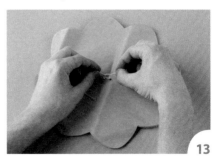

4. Gather each layer of tissue paper toward center on opposite side of knot (photo 14).

5. Once all layers are gathered, start pulling layers down one by one—starting with outside layer—to form carnation flower shape.

Tips: Use different sizes of Spellbinders™ circular dies to create small and large flowers. Create multicolored flowers by using different colors of tissue paper together.

Using Die Templates as Stencils

To get a great finished look, try this fun technique!

1. Die-cut and emboss cardstock with die template.

2. Leave cardstock in die template with cut edge down.

3. Apply ink or chalk to cardstock through open areas of die template (photo 15).

4. Remove cardstock from die template (photo 16).

Tips: Use an airbrush marker system to lightly color embossed areas. Spellbinders™ Nestabilities® die templates allow for an uncolored border around the die cut. Other Spellbinders™ die template shapes allow for colored, embossed features, depending on the shapes and images within the die template.

Floret

Create beautiful paper florets with these easy steps.

1. Using a border die template such as Floral Doily Accents die template, die-cut a 6-inch-long border from cardstock.

2. With long edge horizontal on work surface, score vertical lines every ¼ inch (photo 17).

3. Accordion-fold strip along scored lines (photo 18).

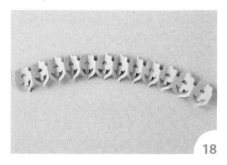

4. Overlap short ends of scored border to form a ring and adhere in place; let dry completely. Press accordion-folded ring flat and attach to project, using adhesive dots (photo 19).

Cake-Stand Pillar

Use this easy-to-make design to create a handy cake-stand pillar or whip up unique holiday treat wraps made with colorful cardstock.

1. Using #2 Grand Scalloped Rectangles die template, die-cut a scalloped rectangle from thin cardboard (photo 20).

2. With short edge horizontal on work surface, score vertical lines along bottom edge of scallops on each long edge as shown (photo 21).

3. Referring to photo, cut off one short scalloped edge and two scallops off long edges (photo 22).

4. To form tabs, cut slits between each scallop on long edges (photo 23).

5. Apply double-sided tape on printed side of thin cardboard along straight edge. Roll rectangle into a tube and adhere short edges together (photo 24).

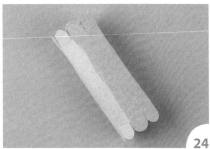

6. Wrap and adhere a 3¼ x 6-inch piece of desired color cardstock around pillar (photo 25).

7. Push tabs toward center of post (photo 26). ▪

Did You Know?

Spellbinders™ die templates can be used to cut many different mediums, such as cardstock, felt, thin cardboard and tissue paper to name a few.

Ice Cream & Cake Party Set

DESIGNS BY **KIMBERLY CRAWFORD**

Banner

Using #5 Classic Scalloped Circles LG die template, die-cut and emboss five scalloped circles from Rad Plaid paper.

Using #5 Standard Circles LG die template, die-cut and emboss five circles from Teal/Canary paper.

Using small cone Nested Ice Cream Cones die template, die-cut and emboss five cones from Road Map paper. In the same manner, die-cut and emboss five small scoops of ice cream from Betty Bird paper.

Referring to photo, layer and adhere die cuts to create banner pieces.

Thread a button with twine; tie bow on front; trim ends. Repeat with remaining buttons. Using adhesive dots, attach a button to top of each ice cream cone.

Adhere stickers to banner pieces to spell "Party."

Punch two holes through top of each banner piece. Thread banner pieces onto ribbon as shown. Cut a V-notch at each end of ribbon.

Sources: *Printed papers from Echo Park Paper Co.; stickers from American Crafts Inc.; die templates and die-cutting/embossing machine from Spellbinders™ Paper Arts; paper adhesive from SCRAPBOOK ADHESIVES BY 3L™.*

- Printed papers: Little Girl Betty Bird, Little Girl Teal/Canary, Little Boy Road Map, Little Boy Rad Plaid
- White Puffy Chit Chat letter stickers
- 5 yellow buttons
- White twine
- 36 inches ½-inch-wide yellow/white polka-dot ribbon
- Spellbinders™ Nestabilities® die templates: Standard Circles LG (#S4-114), Classic Scalloped Circles LG (#S4-124)
- Spellbinders™ Nested Ice Cream Cones Shapeabilities® die templates (#S4-275)
- Spellbinders™ Grand Calibur® machine
- ⅛-inch hole punch
- Adhesive dots
- Paper adhesive

Cake Stand

Project note: When applying adhesive, use a large amount to ensure a strong bond between die-cut pieces.

Referring to Cake-Stand Pillar technique and using #2 Grand Scalloped Rectangles die template, die-cut and form a pillar from thin cardboard. Repeat for bottom pillar using #4 Grand Scalloped Rectangles die template.

Using #3 Grand Circles die template, die-cut and emboss two circles from thin cardboard and a circle from Jody's Stripe paper. In the same manner, die-cut and emboss two #7 circles from thin cardboard and a circle from Danielle Doily paper. Adhere matching-size cardboard circles together.

Using Big Scalloped Border Grand die template, die-cut and emboss two borders from Sally Stitches paper and two borders from Rad Plaid paper. Score a horizontal line ¼ inch below straight edge on each border. Cut slits from straight edge to score line every ¼–½ inch along length of each border. **Note:** *Do not cut past score line.* Apply adhesive around edge of one layered cardboard circle and adhere a border in place by aligning scored line with edge of circle and folding over snipped edge. Repeat for second layered circle.

Adhere paper circles to tops of cardboard circles, creating two plates for cake stand.

Referring to photo, layer and adhere cake-stand pillars and plates together as shown.

Sources: Cardstock from Bazzill Basics Paper Inc.; printed papers from Echo Park Paper Co.; die templates and die-cutting/embossing machine from Spellbinders™ Paper Arts; double-sided adhesive from Scor-Pal Products.

- Yellow cardstock
- Thin cardboard (cereal boxes)
- Printed papers: Little Girl Danielle Doily, Little Girl Jody's Stripe, Little Girl Sally Stitches, Little Boy Rad Plaid
- Spellbinders™ Nestabilities® die templates: Grand Circles (#LF-114), Grand Scalloped Rectangles (#LF-133)
- Spellbinders™ Big Scalloped Border Grand Borderabilities® die template (#S7-018)
- Spellbinders™ Grand Calibur® machine
- Scoring tool
- Double-sided adhesive

Did You Know?

You can use Nestabilities® die templates to cut one-of-a-kind shaped cards and favors for your party sets.

Cupcake Picks

Materials

- Printed papers: Little Girl Betty Bird, Little Boy Road Map
- ½-inch-wide green/white polka-dot ribbon
- Bamboo skewers
- Spellbinders™ Nested Ice Cream Cones Shapeabilities® die templates (#S4-275)
- Spellbinders™ Grand Calibur® machine
- Scoring tool
- Paper adhesive

Using small cone die template, die-cut and emboss six cones from Road Map paper. Die-cut and emboss six small ice cream scoops from Betty Bird paper.

Score a vertical line down middle of each die cut. Fold along scored lines with right sides facing.

Adhere one-half of a scored cone to back of one-half of another scored cone. Continue to adhere all cones together. Repeat with scored ice cream scoops.

Trim skewer to desired length. Referring to photo, slide ice cream scoops and cones onto skewer and secure in place with adhesive as needed.

Cut a 10-inch length of ribbon. Tie a bow around skewer below ice cream cone; V-notch ribbon ends.

Repeat instructions as needed for desired number of cupcake picks.

Sources: Printed papers from Echo Park Paper Co.; ribbon from Creative Impressions Inc.; die templates and die-cutting/embossing machine from Spellbinders™ Paper Arts; paper adhesive from Scor-Pal Products.

Ice Cream Cone Wrappers

Using #7 Grand Circles die template, die-cut and emboss a circle from Betty Bird paper. **Note:** *One circle will form three wrappers.*

Fold circle in half three times; unfold circle. The circle should be divided into eight pie-shaped sections. Cut one piece from circle containing two and one-third pie pieces. With desired side facing out, fold piece along scored lines and adhere short flap to inside, forming wrapper. Cut two more pieces from circle to create two more wrappers.

Materials

- Printed papers: Little Girl Betty Bird, Little Boy Rad Plaid, Little Girl Teal/Canary
- Spellbinders™ Nestabilities® die templates: Grand Circles (#LF-114), Classic Scalloped Circles SM (#S4-125), Standard Circles LG (#S4-114), Classic Heart (#S4-136)
- Spellbinders™ Grand Calibur® machine
- Scoring tool
- Double-sided tape

Using #1 Classic Scalloped Circles SM die template, die-cut and emboss three scalloped circles from Rad Plaid paper. Using #1 Standard Circles LG die template, die-cut and emboss three circles from Teal/Canary paper. Using #1 Classic Heart die template, die-cut and emboss three hearts from Teal/Canary paper. Layer and adhere die cuts to wrappers as shown. ■

Sources: Printed papers from Echo Park Paper Co.; die templates and die-cutting/embossing machine from Spellbinders™ Paper Arts; double-sided tape from Scor-Pal Products.

Easter Party

DESIGNS BY **LESLEY LANGDON & TINA MCDONALD**
DIAGRAMS ON PAGE 63

Basket

Using #6 Grand Big Scalloped Ovals die template, die-cut and emboss a scalloped oval from printed paper.

Referring to diagram on page 63, score and cut scalloped oval. With oval positioned as in diagram, fold top and bottom center pieces in at scored lines forming front and back of basket. Referring to photo, fold side panels up and adhere corner pieces to body of basket.

Cut two 8½ x ¾-inch pieces from printed paper. Adhere to basket as shown forming crisscrossed basket handles.

In the same manner as for Place Card (page 14), create a guest's name banner. Attach banner to basket using foam squares. Embellish with gems.

Sources: *Cardstock from Bazzill Basics Paper Inc.; printed paper from Graphic 45; distress ink pad from Ranger Industries Inc.; self-adhesive gems from Want2Scrap; die templates and die-cutting/embossing machine from Spellbinders™ Paper Arts; foam squares and paper adhesive from SCRAPBOOK ADHESIVES BY 3L™.*

Materials

- White cardstock
- Once Upon a Springtime Fairy Folk printed paper
- Pink distress ink pad
- Black fine-tip marker
- 2 large pink self-adhesive gems
- Spellbinders™ Grand Big Scalloped Ovals Nestabilities® die templates (#LF-251)
- Spellbinders™ Ribbon Banners Shapeabilities® die templates (#S4-324)
- Spellbinders™ Grand Calibur® machine
- Scoring tool
- Craft sponge
- Adhesive foam squares
- Paper adhesive

Materials

- White cardstock
- Once Upon a Springtime printed papers: Once Upon a Springtime, Butterfly Kisses
- Pink distress ink pad
- Black fine-tip marker
- 2 large pink self-adhesive gems
- Spellbinders™ Grand Scalloped Circles Nestabilities® die templates (#LF-124)
- Spellbinders™ Ribbon Banners Shapeabilities® die templates (#S4-324)
- Spellbinders™ Grand Calibur® machine
- Craft sponge
- Hot-glue gun
- Adhesive foam squares
- Paper adhesive
- Computer with printer (optional)

Napkin Holder

Using #2 Grand Scalloped Circles die template, die-cut and emboss a scalloped circle from Butterfly Kisses paper. In the same manner, die-cut and emboss a #1 scalloped circle from Once Upon a Springtime paper. Layer and adhere die cuts together, applying adhesive to center of small scalloped circle only.

Wrap layered die cuts into a tube and secure ends together with hot glue. Apply adhesive as needed to adhere edges of small circle.

In the same manner as for Place Card (page 14), create a guest's name banner. Attach banner to napkin holder using foam squares. Apply hot glue to foam squares as needed to secure banner in place. Embellish with gems.

Sources: *Cardstock from Bazzill Basics Paper Inc.; printed papers from Graphic 45; distress ink pad from Ranger Industries Inc.; self-adhesive gems from Want2Scrap; die templates and die-cutting/embossing machine from Spellbinders™ Paper Arts; hot-glue gun from Glue Arts; foam squares from SCRAPBOOK ADHESIVES BY 3L™.*

Did You Know?

Spellbinders™ die templates are the only dies that provide triple function—cut, emboss and stencil.

Materials

- White cardstock
- Once Upon a Springtime printed papers: Once Upon a Springtime, Woodland Fantasy
- Pink distress ink pad
- Black fine-tip marker
- 2 large pink self-adhesive gems
- Spellbinders™ Grand Scalloped Circles Nestabilities® die templates (#LF-124)
- Spellbinders™ Ribbon Banners Shapeabilities® die templates (#S4-324)
- Spellbinders™ Grand Calibur® machine
- Scoring tool
- Craft sponge
- Adhesive foam squares
- Repositionable tape
- Paper adhesive
- Computer with printer (optional)

Place Card

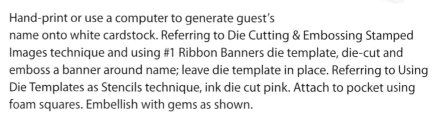

Using #6 Grand Scalloped Circles die template, die-cut and emboss a scalloped circle from Once Upon a Springtime paper. Referring to diagram on page 63, score and cut lower part from scalloped circle. Fold in sides of upper part along scored lines toward center as shown. Adhere as needed to form a 3 x 4⅜-inch place card pocket.

Cut a 2½ x 3⅜-inch piece from Woodland Fantasy paper. Insert inside pocket.
Option: *Write a personal note on desired paper instead of using printed paper.*

Hand-print or use a computer to generate guest's name onto white cardstock. Referring to Die Cutting & Embossing Stamped Images technique and using #1 Ribbon Banners die template, die-cut and emboss a banner around name; leave die template in place. Referring to Using Die Templates as Stencils technique, ink die cut pink. Attach to pocket using foam squares. Embellish with gems as shown.

Form a 3 x 3¾-inch top-folded card from white cardstock. Adhere place card to card front.

Sources: *Cardstock from Bazzill Basics Paper Inc.; printed papers from Graphic 45; distress ink pad from Ranger Industries Inc.; self-adhesive gems from Want2Scrap; die templates and die-cutting/embossing machine from Spellbinders™ Paper Arts; foam squares from SCRAPBOOK ADHESIVES BY 3L™; paper adhesive from Beacon Adhesives Inc.*

Funnel of Fun

Using #6 Grand Scalloped Circles die template, die-cut and emboss a scalloped circle from printed paper.

Wrap scalloped circle to form a cone shape as shown; adhere using hot glue.

In the same manner as for Place Card (above), create a guest's name banner. Attach banner to cone using foam squares. Embellish with gems. ■

Sources: *Cardstock from Bazzill Basics Paper Inc.; printed paper from Graphic 45; distress ink pad from Ranger Industries Inc.; self-adhesive gems from Want2Scrap; die templates and die-cutting/embossing machine from Spellbinders™ Paper Arts; hot-glue gun from Glue Arts; foam squares from SCRAPBOOK ADHESIVES BY 3L™.*

Materials

- White cardstock
- Once Upon a Springtime printed paper
- Pink distress ink pad
- Black fine-tip marker
- 2 large pink self-adhesive gems
- Spellbinders™ Grand Scalloped Circles Nestabilities® die templates (#LF-124)
- Spellbinders™ Ribbon Banners Shapeabilities® die templates (#S4-324)
- Spellbinders™ Grand Calibur® machine
- Hot-glue gun
- Craft sponge
- Adhesive foam squares
- Paper adhesive
- Computer with printer (optional)

Baby Shower

DESIGNS BY **KAZAN CLARK**

Pompom

Referring to Tissue-Paper Carnation technique and using #5 Grand Dahlia die template, die-cut a dahlia from layered sheets of tissue paper. When gathering

layers, gather half of the layers in one direction and other half in opposite direction. Fluff finished pompom to create a fuller shape. ***Note:*** *Use more layers of tissue paper to create a fuller pompom.*

Sources: Die templates and die-cutting/embossing machine from Spellbinders™ Paper Arts.

Materials

- Tissue paper: pink or light blue
- White string
- Spellbinders™ Grand Dahlia Nestabilities® die templates (#LF-191)
- Spellbinders™ Grand Calibur® machine
- ⅛-inch hole punch

Favor Box

Using Square Petal Top Box die template, die-cut and emboss a box from white cardstock. Score, cut and fold box following manufacturer's instructions.

Cut four 2⅝ x 1¼-inch pieces from desired printed paper. Adhere a piece to each side of box.

To create flower topper, follow Tissue-Paper Carnation technique and use #3 Dahlia die template and tissue paper to create a 16-layer carnation.

Wrap ends of string from bottom of carnation around center of gingham ribbon; tie a knot and trim ends of string. Wrap gingham ribbon around box as shown and secure ends to bottom of box with tape.

Form a bow from satin ribbon; trim ends at an angle. Clip two lengths from pearl spray. Use fishing line to attach baby bottle and pearl spray lengths to ribbon bow. Adhere bow to box.

Sources: Printed papers from Echo Park Paper Co.; favors from Wilton Industries; die templates and die-cutting/embossing machine from Spellbinders™ Paper Arts; paper adhesive from SCRAPBOOK ADHESIVES BY 3L™.

Materials

- White cardstock
- Printed papers: Little Girl Gingham Gaby, Little Boy Journaling Cards
- Tissue paper: pink, light blue
- Mini Baby Bottle Favor Accents: pink, light blue
- Pearl spray: pink, light blue
- ⅜-inch-wide gingham ribbon: 8¾ inches light blue, 8¾ inches pink
- White string
- Fishing line
- Spellbinders™ Nestabilities® die templates: Grand Square Petal Top Box (LF-012), Dahlia (S4-191)
- Spellbinders™ Grand Calibur® machine
- ⅛-inch hole punch
- Tape
- Paper adhesive

Invitation

Form a 5½ x 5-inch top-folded card from white cardstock. Following Making a Shaped Card technique, die-cut and emboss a card using #4 Fleur de Lis Rectangles die template.

Using #5 Classic Rectangles LG die template, die-cut and emboss a rectangle from Journaling Cards paper. Adhere to card front.

Using #4 Labels Fourteen die template, die-cut and emboss a label from Gingham Gaby paper. Adhere to card front.

Hand-print or use a computer to generate invitation text. Referring to Die Cutting & Embossing Stamped Images technique and using #3 Labels Fourteen die template, die-cut and emboss label around text.

- White cardstock
- Printed papers; Little Girl Gingham Gaby, Little Boy Journaling Cards
- Black fine-tip marker
- 3 inches ⅜-inch-wide light blue gingham ribbon
- White string
- 2 pink buttons
- Spellbinders™ Nestabilities® die templates: Fleur de Lis Rectangles (#S4-317), Classic Rectangles LG (#S4-132), Labels Fourteen (#S4-290)
- Spellbinders™ Grand Calibur® machine
- Adhesive dimensional dots
- Repositionable tape
- Paper adhesive
- Computer with printer (optional)

Trim ends of ribbon at an angle. Adhere to card front as shown. Using dimensional dots, attach invitation label to card front.

Insert string through buttons; tie knots on back; trim ends. Attach to card front as shown using dimensional dots.

Sources: Printed papers from Echo Park Paper Co.; die templates and die-cutting/embossing machine from Spellbinders™ Paper Arts; dimensional dots from Glue Dots; paper adhesive from SCRAPBOOK ADHESIVES BY 3L™.

- Cardstock: white, light blue
- 2¾ x 2¼-inch baby photo
- Black fine-tip marker
- Buttons: 1 pink, 1 blue
- Spellbinders™ Nestabilities® die templates: Fleur de Lis Rectangles (#S4-317), Classic Rectangles LG (#S4-132)
- Spellbinders™ Grand Calibur® machine
- Adhesive dots
- Repositionable tape
- Paper adhesive
- Computer with printer (optional)

Announcement

Follow first paragraph of Invitation instructions (above) to create a 5½ x 5-inch top-folded die-cut card.

Hand-print or use a computer to generate announcement text onto light blue cardstock. In the same manner as for invitation and using #5 Classic Rectangles LG die template, die-cut and emboss a rectangle around text, referring to photo for positioning. Adhere to card front.

Using dimensional dots, attach photo to card front. In the same manner, attach buttons to card front.

Sources: Die templates and die-cutting/embossing machine from Spellbinders™ Paper Arts; adhesive dots from Glue Dots; paper adhesive from SCRAPBOOK ADHESIVES BY 3L™.

Double the love, laughter, and fun
Two Special lives have just begun

A
Shower
for
Two

- White cardstock
- Printed papers: pink glitter, light blue glitter, Little Girl Gingham Gaby, Little Boy Journaling Cards
- White glitter cardstock alphabet stickers
- Light blue tissue paper
- Pink ribbon: 10 inches ⅜-inch-wide gingham, 39 inches ⅝-inch-wide satin
- Various pink and blue buttons
- White string
- Spellbinders™ Dahlia Nestabilities® die templates (#S4-191)
- Spellbinders™ Shapeabilities® die templates: Nested Pennants (#S5-028), Nested Lacey Pennants (#S5-029)
- Spellbinders™ Grand Calibur® machine
- Adhesive dimensional dots
- Adhesive dots
- Paper adhesive

Banner

Project note: *Die-cut as many pennants and flowers as needed to spell out desired sentiment.*

Using #4 Nested Lacey Pennants, die-cut and emboss three lacey pennants from light blue glitter paper and two lacey pennants from pink glitter paper.

Using #4 Nested Pennants die template, die-cut five pennants from white cardstock. Die-cut two #3 pennants from Gingham Gaby paper and three from Journaling Cards paper. Layer and adhere pennants together as shown.

Using #3 Dahlia die template, die-cut two flowers from pink glitter paper and three flowers from light blue glitter paper. Attach flowers to pennants as shown with dimensional dots.

Attach alphabet stickers to flowers to spell out "TWiNS." Using adhesive dots, attach buttons to pennants as shown.

Adhere pennants to satin ribbon as shown.

Following Tissue-Paper Carnation technique and using #3 Dahlia die template and tissue paper, create two 16-layer carnations.

Cut gingham ribbon into two 5-inch lengths; cut a V-notch at each end. Tie a carnation to middle of each length of ribbon; trim thread ends. Tie to each side of pennants as shown. ■

Sources: Printed papers from Echo Park Paper Co.; alphabet stickers from American Crafts Inc.; die templates and die-cutting/embossing machine from Spellbinders™ Paper Arts; adhesive dots from Glue Dots; paper adhesive from SCRAPBOOK ADHESIVES BY 3L™.

Mother's Day

DESIGNS BY **MONA PENDLETON**

Project note: *Use black ink to stamp images; sponge light brown ink onto edges of pieces as desired.*

Magnet

Stamp "World's Best Mom" onto cream cardstock. Referring to Die Cutting & Embossing Stamped Images technique and using #1 Standard Circles LG die template, die-cut and emboss a circle around sentiment.

Stamp small flower onto cream cardstock; color using markers. In the same manner as before, die-cut and emboss image using #2 Blossom Three die template. Attach sentiment circle to flower with foam squares.

Referring to Floret technique, form a floret using a 12 x 1-inch piece of Soiree Words paper. Adhere flower to floret.

Using #3 Blossom Three die template, die-cut and emboss a flower from green cardstock. Adhere to back of floret.

Using #1 Nested Lacey Pennants die template, die-cut and emboss a ribbon from cream cardstock; do not remove template. Referring to Using Die Templates as Stencils technique and using RV17 marker and airbrush system, ink die-cut ribbon pink. Repeat for a second die-cut ribbon. Adhere to back of green flower as shown.

Cut satin and polka-dot ribbons in half; cut a V-notch at one end of each length. Layer and adhere ribbons to back of green flower as shown.

Cut a 1½ x 1¼-inch piece from magnet sheet. Adhere to back of flower.

Sources: *Cardstock from Bazzill Basics Paper Inc. and WorldWin Papers; printed paper from Pink Paislee; stamp set from JustRite Stampers®; markers and airbrush system from Imagination International Inc.; die templates and die-cutting/embossing machine from Spellbinders™ Paper Arts; foam squares and paper adhesive from SCRAPBOOK ADHESIVES BY 3L™.*

Materials

- Cardstock: green, cream
- Soiree Words printed paper
- You Are the Best stamp set
- Dye ink pads: black, light brown distress
- Copic® markers: RV11, RV17
- Self-adhesive magnet sheet
- Ribbon: 6 inches ⅝-inch-wide green satin, 5 inches ⅜-inch-wide pink/white polka-dot
- Spellbinders™ Nestabilities® die templates: Standard Circles LG (#S4-114), Blossom Three (#S4-312)
- Spellbinders™ Nested Lacey Pennants Shapeabilities® die template (#S5-029)
- Spellbinders™ Grand Calibur® machine
- Airbrush system
- Craft sponge
- Scoring tool
- Adhesive foam squares
- Repositionable tape
- Paper adhesive

Gift Tag

Stamp "Made just for You …" onto cream cardstock. In the same manner as for Magnet (above) and using #2 Standard Circles LG die template, die-cut and emboss a circle around words.

Stamp large flower onto cream cardstock and color with markers. In the same manner as before, die-cut and emboss image using #3 Blossom Three die template. Attach sentiment circle to flower with foam squares.

Referring to instructions for magnet, create a floret using two 12 x 1⅜-inch pieces of Soiree Words paper. ***Note:*** *Adhere pieces together forming a 24 x 1⅜-inch strip.* Adhere flower to floret.

Using #4 Blossom Three die template, die-cut and emboss

Materials

- Cardstock: green, cream
- Soiree Words printed paper
- Stamp sets: You Are the Best, Charmed
- Dye ink pads: black, light brown distress
- Copic markers: RV11, RV17, YG03
- Ribbon: 8 inches ⅝-inch-wide green satin, 12 inches ¾-inch-wide pink/white polka-dot, 20 inches ⅝-inch-wide white satin
- Spellbinders™ Nestabilities® die templates: Standard Circles LG (#S4-114), Blossom Three (#S4-312)
- Spellbinders™ Nested Lacey Pennants Shapeabilities® die template (#S5-029)
- Spellbinders™ Grand Calibur® machine
- Airbrush system
- Craft sponge
- Scoring tool
- Adhesive foam squares
- Repositionable tape
- Paper adhesive

a flower from green cardstock. Adhere to back of floret.

In the same manner as for magnet and using #2 Nested Lacey Pennants die template, create two die-cut ribbons. Stamp ribbon outline onto die-cut ribbons. Adhere die-cut ribbons to green flower.

Cut green ribbon in half. Cut two 4-inch lengths from polka-dot ribbon. Cut a V-notch at one end of each length of ribbon. Layer and adhere cut ribbons to flower as shown.

Fold remaining length of polka-dot ribbon in half; adhere both ends to top back of green flower. Thread white ribbon through ribbon loop. Tie a bow around handle of gift bag or attach to package; trim ends.

Sources: Cardstock from Bazzill Basics Paper Inc. and WorldWin Papers; printed paper from Pink Paislee; stamp sets from JustRite Stampers®; markers and airbrush system from Imagination International Inc.; die templates and die-cutting/embossing machine from Spellbinders™ Paper Arts; foam squares and paper adhesive from SCRAPBOOK ADHESIVES BY 3L™.

Card

Form a 4¼ x 5½-inch side-folded card from cream cardstock.

Cut a 4 x 5¼-inch piece from Daily Junque Map paper. Adhere to light brown cardstock; trim a small border. Adhere to card front.

In the same manner as for Gift Tag (page 19), create a layered flower with ribbons (pages 19, 20), stamping "One of a Kind" onto center circle. **Note:** *When creating stamped ribbons, stamp "Mom" on one ribbon.* Adhere flower to card front as shown. ■

Sources: Cardstock from Bazzill Basics Paper Inc. and WorldWin Papers; printed papers from Pink Paislee; stamp set from JustRite Stampers®; markers and airbrush system from Imagination International Inc.; die templates and die-cutting/embossing machine from Spellbinders™ Paper Arts; foam squares and paper adhesive from SCRAPBOOK ADHESIVES BY 3L™.

Materials

- Cardstock: green, cream, light brown
- Printed papers: Soiree Words, Daily Junque Map
- You Are the Best stamp set
- Dye ink pads: black, light brown distress
- Copic markers: RV11, RV17, YG03
- Self-adhesive magnet sheet
- Ribbon: 8 inches ⅝-inch-wide green satin, 7 inches ¾-inch-wide pink/white polka-dot
- Spellbinders™ Nestabilities® die templates: Standard Circles LG (#S4-114), Blossom Three (#S4-312)
- Spellbinders™ Nested Lacey Pennants Shapeabilities® die template (#S5-029)
- Spellbinders™ Grand Calibur® machine
- Airbrush system
- Craft sponge
- Adhesive foam squares
- Paper adhesive

Made just for You...

One of a Kind

Mom

4923

World's Best Mom

Bridal Shower

DESIGNS BY **BECCA FEEKEN**

Menu Pocket Card

Hand-print with fine-tip marker or use a computer to generate menu text onto pink cardstock. Referring to Die Cutting & Embossing Stamped Images technique and using #3 Grand Labels One die template, die-cut and emboss a label around text.

Cut a 12 x 12-inch sheet of printed paper in half, creating two 6 x 12-inch strips. Fold one strip in half creating a 6 x 6-inch top-folded card; set aside.

For card pocket, place remaining 6 x 12-inch strip on work surface with long side horizontal; score vertical lines 1 and 1⅛ inches from left edge. At opposite end of strip, die-cut and emboss a decorative edge referring to Selective Die Cutting technique and using #4 Grand Labels Four die template. **Note:** *Save die-cut scrap to be used later on flatware caddy.*

Using large Lotus Pendants die template, die-cut and emboss a pendant from white cardstock. Referring to photo, adhere pendant to inside of decorative edge on pocket piece. Wrap seam binding around pocket and tie a bow as shown; trim ends.

Fold pocket piece along scored lines and adhere to card front applying adhesive along bottom flap only. Secure top corners of pocket front with adhesive dots.

Referring to Floret technique and using Floral Doily Accents die template, die-cut a 6-inch-long border from pink pearlescent cardstock and form a floret. Attach floret to menu pocket as shown using adhesive dots.

Adhere paper rose to floret. Slide menu inside pocket.

Sources: *Cardstock from Core'dinations and Bazzill Basics Paper Inc.; printed paper from Advantus Corp./The Girls' Paperie; die templates and die-cutting/embossing machine from Spellbinders™ Paper Arts; adhesive dots and paper adhesive from Glue Dots.*

Materials

- Cardstock: pink, white, pink pearlescent
- Vintage Whimsy Cottage Vine printed paper
- Black fine-tip marker
- Pink paper rose
- 35 inches ½-inch-wide cream seam binding
- Spellbinders™ Nestabilities® die templates: Grand Labels One (#LF-161), Grand Labels Four (#LF-190)
- Spellbinders™ Shapeabilities® die templates: Lotus Pendants (#S4-269), Floral Doily Accents (#S5-040)
- Spellbinders™ Grand Calibur® machine
- Scoring tool
- Adhesive dots
- Repositionable tape
- Paper adhesive
- Computer with printer (optional)

Menu

Ms. Noelle Green

Materials

- Cardstock: white, pink pearlescent
- Vintage Whimsy Cottage Vine printed paper
- Black fine-tip marker
- Pink paper rose
- 19 inches ½-inch-wide cream seam binding
- Spellbinders™ Nestabilities® die templates: Long Classic Rectangles LG (#S4-142), Grand Labels Four (#LF-190)
- Spellbinders™ Shapeabilities® die templates: Lotus Pendants (#S4-269), Floral Doily Accents (#S5-040)
- Spellbinders™ Grand Calibur® machine
- Scoring tool
- Craft knife
- Tape
- Adhesive dots
- Paper adhesive
- Computer with printer (optional)

Place Card & Holder

Hand-print or use a computer to generate guest's name onto white cardstock. In the same manner as for Menu Pocket Card (page 22) and using #3 Classic Long Rectangles LG die template, die-cut and emboss a rectangle around guest's name, forming a place card. Adhere to pink pearlescent cardstock; trim a border. Tie a triple bow with seam binding; cut a V-notch at each end of seam binding and adhere to place card.

Using #4 Grand Labels Four die template, die-cut and emboss a label from printed paper. With long edge horizontal on work surface, score vertical lines ¾ inch, 1¼ inches, 3¾ inches, 6¼ inches and 6¾ inches from left edge. Cut a 4-inch slit centered in the score line created at 3¾ inches.

Valley-fold first two scored lines. Mountain-fold next scored line so that slit is at the top of the holder. Mountain-fold next two lines; first folded section will be card holder base; second section will be adhered inside of place card holder with bottom edges aligned. **Note:** *If you want place card holder to be weighted down for more stability, glue several pennies to reverse side of front before adhering.*

Using large Lotus Pendants die template, die-cut and emboss a pendant from white cardstock. Slide pendant die cut into slit in top fold of place card holder; secure inside with tape.

In the same manner as for Menu Pocket Card, create a floret. Attach floret to place card holder as shown using adhesive dots. Adhere paper flower to floret. Set place card in place card holder.

Sources: *Cardstock from Core'dinations and Bazzill Basics Paper Inc.; printed paper from Advantus Corp./The Girls' Paperie; die templates and die-cutting/embossing machine from Spellbinders™ Paper Arts; adhesive dots and paper adhesive from Glue Dots.*

Did You Know?

Adding a small piece of removable tape will keep your die template in the exact place you want it while cutting and embossing.

Flatware Caddy

Using #6 Grand Labels Four die template, die-cut and emboss a label from printed paper. Score and cut lines on label as shown on pattern below. Fold in along scored lines to form a flatware caddy, folding up short flap last.

Using large Lotus Pendants die template, die-cut and emboss a pendant from white cardstock. Referring to photo, adhere to backside of short flap, trimming off petals of pendant as needed.

In the same manner as for Menu Pocket Card (page 22), create a floret. Attach floret to flatware caddy as shown using adhesive dots. Adhere paper rose to floret.

Using accent Classic Scalloped Borderabilities Petite die template, die-cut and emboss a 6⅝ x 1½-inch border from white cardstock. Place die-cut scrap piece from Menu Pocket Card centered on top edge of white cardstock border folding piece over edge as shown; adhere in place. With long edge horizontal on work surface, score vertical lines 1 inch and 4 inches from left edge. Wrap around flatware caddy as shown, aligning scored edges with sides of caddy; overlap and secure ends together on back.

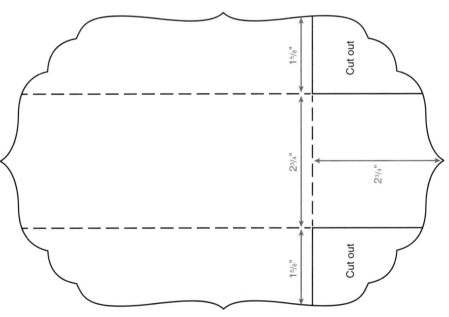

Materials

- Cardstock: white, pink pearlescent
- Vintage Whimsy Cottage Vine printed paper
- Pink paper rose
- 23 inches ½-inch-wide cream seam binding
- Spellbinders™ Grand Labels Four Nestabilities® die templates (#LF-190)
- Spellbinders™ Shapeabilities® die templates: Lotus Pendants (#S4-269), Floral Doily Accents (#S5-040)
- Spellbinders™ Classic Scalloped Borderabilities® Petite die templates (#S4-239)
- Spellbinders™ Grand Calibur® machine
- Scoring tool
- Craft knife
- Tape
- Adhesive dots
- Paper adhesive

Referring to photo, wrap seam binding around flatware caddy, tie bow on front and cut a V-notch at each end of seam binding. Secure as needed with adhesive dots.

Place flatware in caddy.

Sources: Cardstock from Core'dinations and Bazzill Basics Paper Inc.; printed paper from Advantus Corp./The Girls' Paperie; die templates and die-cutting/embossing machine from Spellbinders™ Paper Arts; adhesive dots and paper adhesive from Glue Arts.

1⅝"
Cut out
2¾"
2¾"
1⅝"
Cut out

Bridal Shower Flatware Caddy
Cut along solid lines; score along dashed lines

Garden Party Set

DESIGNS BY **JULIE OVERBY & KAREN TAYLOR**

Invitation

Form a 5 x 7-inch side-folded card from cream cardstock. Cut a 4¾ x 6¾-inch piece from Noteworthy paper and a 4 x 6-inch piece from Table Cloth paper; ink edges brown. Layer and adhere to card front as shown.

Hand-print or use a computer to generate garden party invitation onto Lace Stripes paper. Trim down to a 3 x 3⅞-inch piece. Center and adhere to card front.

Referring to Making Frames technique and using #4 and #5 Labels Eighteen die templates, die-cut and emboss a frame from Red/Cream paper; ink edges brown. Referring to photo, attach frame to card front using foam squares.

Using #4 Rose Creations die template, die-cut and emboss a flower from Stamp of Approval paper; ink brown. Die-cut and emboss #5 flower from Green/Green paper; ink brown. Lay each flower facedown onto a foam pad; gently rub petals using a scoring tool, making petals curl. Layer and adhere flowers together, applying adhesive to center of flowers only. Attach to card front using foam square. Embellish flower with gem.

Sources: *Cardstock from WorldWin Papers; printed papers from Echo Park Paper Co.; chalk ink pad from Clearsnap Inc.; self-adhesive gem from Want2Scrap; die templates and die-cutting/embossing machine from Spellbinders™ Paper Arts; foam squares from SCRAPBOOK ADHESIVES BY 3L™.*

Materials

- Cream cardstock
- For the Record printed papers: Noteworthy, Table Cloth, Lace Stripes, Stamp of Approval, Red/Cream, Green/Green
- Brown chalk ink pad
- Black fine-tip marker
- Large black self-adhesive gem
- Spellbinders™ Labels Eighteen Nestabilities® die templates (#S4-310)
- Spellbinders™ Rose Creations Shapeabilities® die templates (#S5-050)
- Spellbinders™ Grand Calibur® machine
- Scoring tool
- Foam pad
- Adhesive foam squares
- Repositionable tape
- Paper adhesive
- Computer with printer (optional)

IT'S A GARDEN PARTY!!

WHERE: WISTERIA GARDENS
TEA HOUSE
WHEN: SAT. JUNE 29TH
WHAT: GIRLS ONLY PARTY
RSVP: 444-321-3333

Did You Know?

You can create fun patterns on your cardstock by embossing multiple die templates. Instead of cutting, try embossing only for endless possibilities!

VAL
JONES

IT'S A GARDEN PARTY!!

WHERE: WISTERIA GARDENS
TEA HOUSE
WHEN: SAT. JUNE 29TH
WHAT: GIRLS ONLY PARTY
RSVP: 444-321-3333

Materials

- For the Record printed papers: Lace Stripes, Stamp of Approval
- Yellow tulle
- Brown chalk ink pad
- Medium-size black self-adhesive gem
- 3¾ inches ⅜-inch-wide black/cream striped ribbon
- Spellbinders™ Nestabilities® die templates: Labels Eighteen (#S4-310), Tear Drop Circles (#S4-344)
- Spellbinders™ Grand Calibur® machine
- Scoring tool
- Tape
- Adhesive dots
- Paper adhesive

Favor Purse

Using #5 Labels Eighteen die template, die-cut and emboss a label from Stamp of Approval paper; ink edges brown. With long edge of label horizontal on work surface, score vertical lines 1¾ inches, 2⅛ inches and 2½ inches from left edge. Referring to photo, fold along scored lines to form purse base.

Using #2 Tear Drop Circles die template, die-cut and emboss a circle from Lace Stripes paper. Score a line down center of circle and fold in half.

Adhere one half of folded circle to back of purse base as shown. Fold remaining half of circle over front of purse base; do not adhere. Attach gem to purse as shown.

Using adhesive dots, attach ends of ribbon to back of purse to create a handle. Wrap favor in tulle and place favor inside purse. Tape purse closed.

Sources: *Printed papers from Echo Park Paper Co.; chalk ink pad from Clearsnap Inc.; self-adhesive gem from Want2Scrap; die templates and die-cutting/embossing machine from Spellbinders™ Paper Arts; adhesive dots from Glue Dots.*

Place Card

Using #5 Labels Eighteen die template, die-cut and emboss a label from Table Cloth paper to form a place card base. In the same manner as for Invitation (page 26), die-cut and emboss a frame from Stamp of Approval paper using #4 and #3 Labels Eighteen die templates; ink edges brown.

Hand-print or use a computer to generate guest's name onto Lace Stripes paper. Trim down to a 2¼ x 3-inch piece. Center and adhere to place card base. Using foam squares, attach frame to place card as shown.

Using #2 Rose Creations die template, die-cut and emboss a flower from Stamp of Approval paper. Leaving die template in place, refer to Using Die Templates as Stencils technique to ink petals with brown ink. Die-cut and emboss a #3 flower from Green/Green paper; in the same manner, ink petals using die template as a stencil. Remove die cuts from templates and ink edges with

Materials

- White cardboard
- For the Record printed papers: Table Cloth, Lace Stripes, Stamp of Approval, Green/Green
- Brown chalk ink pad
- Black fine-tip marker
- Medium-size black self-adhesive gem
- Spellbinders™ Labels Eighteen Nestabilities® die templates (#S4-310)
- Spellbinders™ Rose Creations Shapeabilities® die templates (#S5-050)
- Spellbinders™ Grand Calibur® machine
- Scoring tool
- Foam pad
- Adhesive foam squares
- Paper adhesive
- Computer with printer (optional)

brown ink. Lay each flower facedown onto a foam pad; gently rub petals using a scoring tool, making petals curl. Layer and adhere flowers to place card, applying adhesive to center of flowers only. Embellish assembled flower with gem.

Cut a ⅞ x 8-inch piece from white cardboard. With long edge horizontal on work surface, score vertical lines 3½ inches, 4 inches and 4½ inches from left edge. Fold in half at center scored line; adhere short edges of strip together, forming an easel for place card. Adhere to back of place card as shown.

Sources: *Printed papers from Echo Park Paper Co.; chalk ink pad from Clearsnap Inc.; self-adhesive gem from Want2Scrap; die templates and die-cutting/embossing machine from Spellbinders™ Paper Arts; foam squares from SCRAPBOOK ADHESIVES BY 3L™.*

Garden Party Lights

Project note: *When attaching paper flowers to lights, do not allow paper to touch bulbs. Do not leave lights unattended when lit.*

Using #3 Dahlia die template, die-cut and emboss 10 flowers from various green printed papers; repeat to cut 10 flowers from red cardstock. Glue red flowers to backs of green flowers. Set aside.

Using #1 Dahlia die template, die-cut and emboss 10 flowers from green cardstock and 10 flowers from cream cardstock.

Ink edges of all die-cut flowers. Use scoring tool to score each flower between each petal. Using score lines as a guide, cut one petal from each flower.

Punch a hole through center of a flower. Wrap flower around plastic base of a light, placing flower below bulb. If end petals will not overlap, use scissors to make hole larger. Repeat for each flower.

On each flower, overlap end petals and secure with glue. Let dry completely. Adhere cream flowers inside red flowers; adhere green flowers to outside bottom of red flowers. Let dry completely.

To attach flowers onto light strand, push a lightbulb through bottom of each flower. ■

Sources: *Cardstock from Donna Salazar Designs; printed papers from Echo Park Paper Co.; chalk ink pad from Clearsnap Inc.; die templates and die-cutting/embossing machine from Spellbinders™ Paper Arts; Zip Dry Paper Glue from Beacon Adhesives Inc.*

Materials

- Cardstock: red, green, cream
- Various For the Record green printed papers
- Brown chalk ink pad
- Clear 10-count light strand
- Spellbinders™ Dahlia Nestabilities® die templates (#S4-191)
- Spellbinders™ Grand Calibur® machine
- Scoring tool
- Hole punch
- Instant-dry paper glue

Father's Day

DESIGNS BY **LATISHA YOAST**

Card

Using #3 Grand Large Labels die template, die-cut and emboss two labels from white cardstock. With long edge of one label horizontal on work surface, score a vertical line ¾ inch from left edge. Apply adhesive to ¾-inch flap and adhere to un-scored label aligning edges. This will create a 4⅜ x 5⅞-inch top-folded card.

Using #2 Grand Circles die template, die-cut and emboss a circle from green cardstock. Adhere to white cardstock. Referring to photo and Selective Die Cutting technique and using #2 Grand Large Labels die template, die-cut and emboss layered cardstock piece. Stamp "Happy Father's Day!" onto label as shown. Attach label to card front using foam squares.

Cut a ⅛ x 2½-inch strip from black cardstock. Referring to photo, adhere to card front.

Using #1 Nested Pennants die template, die-cut and emboss a pennant from light blue cardstock. Attach pennant to black strip as shown with foam squares.

Using #1 and #2 Grand Large Labels die templates and referring to Making Frames technique, die-cut and emboss a frame from black cardstock. Attach to card front with foam squares.

Sources: Cardstock from WorldWin Papers and Bazzill Basics Paper Inc.; stamp set from Flourishes; die templates and die-cutting/embossing machine from Spellbinders™ Paper Arts; foam squares and paper adhesive from SCRAPBOOK ADHESIVES BY 3L™.

Materials

- Cardstock: white, green, black, light blue
- A Man's View stamp set
- Black dye ink pad
- Spellbinders™ Nestabilities® die templates: Grand Large Labels (#LF-168), Grand Circles (#LF-114)
- Spellbinders™ Nested Pennants Shapeabilities® die templates (#S5-028)
- Spellbinders™ Grand Calibur® machine
- Scoring tool
- Repositionable tape
- Adhesive foam squares
- Paper adhesive

Cupcake Toppers

Using #6 Standard Circles LG die template, die-cut and emboss a circle from black cardstock. Die-cut and emboss a #5 circle from green cardstock.

Tape a toothpick to back of green circle. Adhere circles together with foam squares.

Using #2 Nested Pennants die template, die-cut and emboss a pennant from light blue cardstock.

Stamp "dad" onto white cardstock.

Referring to Die Cutting and Embossing Stamp Images technique and a #1 pennant Nested Pennants, die-cut and emboss a pennant around sentiment.

Adhere pennants together using foam dots. Adhere to layered circle with foam squares.

Repeat for additional cupcake toppers.

Sources: Cardstock from WorldWin Papers and Bazzill Basics Paper Inc.; stamp set from Lawn Fawn; die templates and die-cutting/embossing machine from Spellbinders™ Paper Arts; foam squares and paper adhesive from SCRAPBOOK ADHESIVES BY 3L™.

Materials

- Cardstock: white, green, black, light blue
- Smitty's ABC's stamp set
- Black dye ink pad
- Toothpicks
- Spellbinders™ Standard Circles LG Nestabilities® die templates (#S4-114)
- Spellbinders™ Nested Pennants Shapeabilities® die templates (#S5-028)
- Spellbinders™ Grand Calibur® machine
- Tape
- Adhesive foam squares
- Paper adhesive

Tee Times Notebook

Using #5 Grand Scalloped Rectangles die template, die-cut and emboss a scalloped rectangle from black cardstock.

Using #4 Grand Rectangles die template, die-cut and emboss a rectangle from white cardstock. Center and adhere to black scalloped rectangle.

With short edge of layered die cuts horizontal on work surface, score two vertical lines 3⅜ inches and 3¾ inches from left edge, creating a spine. Fold in at scored lines, forming a 3⅜ x 8⅝-inch side-folded notebook cover. Adhere notebook inside.

Using #5 Standard Circles LG die template, die-cut and emboss a circle from green cardstock. Referring to photo, trim circle and adhere to notebook cover as shown.

Cut a ⅛ x 4½-inch strip from black cardstock. Referring to photo, adhere to cover.

Using #1 Nested Pennants die template, die-cut and emboss a pennant from light blue cardstock. Attach pennant to black strip, using foam squares.

Attach stickers to cover to spell "Tee Times."

Materials

- 2½ x 8-inch section of legal notebook
- Cardstock: white, green, black, light blue
- Tiny Type Clear Black Letter stickers
- Spellbinders™ Nestabilities® die templates: Grand Rectangles (#LF-132), Grand Scalloped Rectangles (#LF-133), Standard Circles LG (#S4-114)
- Spellbinders™ Nested Pennants Shapeabilities® die templates (#S5-028)
- Spellbinders™ Grand Calibur® machine
- Scoring tool
- Adhesive foam squares
- Paper adhesive

Sources: *Cardstock from WorldWin Papers and Bazzill Basics Paper Inc.; stickers from Cosmo Cricket; die templates and die-cutting/embossing machine from Spellbinders™ Paper Arts; foam squares and paper adhesive from SCRAPBOOK ADHESIVES BY 3L™.*

Materials

- Light blue cardstock
- Green felt
- Spellbinders™ Nestabilities® die templates: Star Circles (#S4-335), Standard Circles LG (#S4-114)
- Spellbinders™ Grand Calibur® machine
- Paper adhesive

Coasters

Using #4 Star Circles die template, die-cut and emboss a star circle from light blue cardstock.

Using #5 Standard Circles LG die template, die-cut a circle from felt. Center and adhere to star circle die cut.

Repeat for additional coasters. ■

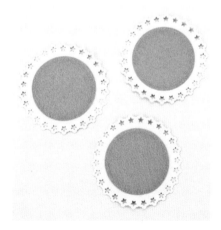

Sources: *Cardstock from Bazzill Basics Paper Inc.; die templates and die-cutting/embossing machine from Spellbinders™ Paper Arts; paper adhesive from SCRAPBOOK ADHESIVES BY 3L™.*

Anniversary Set

DESIGNS BY **TINA MCDONALD**

Invitation

Using #6 Grand Labels Eleven die template, die-cut and emboss a label from cream cardstock, forming a card base. With short edge horizontal on work surface, score a horizontal line 2 inches below top edge. Fold top portion down forming a flap.

Using #5 Grand Labels Eleven die template, die-cut and emboss a label from black cardstock. Cut off top 1¾ inches from black label. Adhere 1¾-inch piece to folded top flap of card base as shown. Adhere remaining piece of black label to card base, aligning straight edge with scored line.

Hand-print or use a computer to generate invitation information onto cream cardstock. Stamp a flourish below text. Referring to Die Cutting & Embossing Stamped Images technique and using #3 Grand Labels Eleven die template, die-cut and emboss a label around invitation information as shown. Cut off top 1 inch from invitation label; 1-inch piece will not be used. In the same manner as before, adhere remaining piece to card base. Attach pearl to center of flourish.

Fold top flap over top of invitation label as shown and adhere.

Referring to Selective Die Cutting technique and using #4 Grand Labels Eleven die template, die-cut and emboss a label from a 5½ x 1¾-inch strip of gray/cream paper. Adhere to top flap as shown; trim top edge as needed before adhering.

Using #2 Lacey Ovals die template, die-cut and emboss an oval from black cardstock. Referring to photo, adhere oval to card base.

Using Accent 2 Renaissance Hearts Pendants die template, die-cut and emboss an accent from gold metallic printed paper. Adhere to lacey oval. Pierce a hole through center of gold metallic die cut; insert brad.

Sources: *Cardstock from WorldWin Papers; printed papers from Anna Griffin Inc.; stamp set from Waltzingmouse Stamps; chalk ink pad from Clearsnap Inc.; gold brad from Creative Impressions Inc.; self-adhesive pearl from Want2Scrap; die templates and die-cutting/embossing machine from Spellbinders™ Paper Arts; paper adhesive from Helmar.*

Materials

- Cardstock: cream, black
- Willow printed papers: gray/cream, gold metallic
- Vintage Banners stamp set
- Black chalk ink pad
- Black fine-tip marker
- Small gold brad
- Small white self-adhesive pearl
- Spellbinders™ Nestabilities® die templates: Grand Labels Eleven (#LF-246), Lacey Ovals (#S4-314)
- Spellbinders™ Renaissance Hearts Pendants Shapeabilities® die templates (#S4-206)
- Spellbinders™ Grand Calibur® machine
- Scoring tool
- Paper piercer
- Repositionable tape
- Paper adhesive
- Computer with printer (optional)

50TH ANNIVERSARY
You are invited to help us celebrate the 50th anniversary of
Robert and Susan Smith.
When: Saturday, April 15th 7-9PM
Where: Centerville Community Center
RSVP by April 1 by calling
(403) 443-0091

Materials

- Candle
- Cardstock: cream, black
- Printed papers: Curtain Call, Willow gray/cream, Willow gold metallic
- Small gold brad
- 19 inches 1-inch-wide gold metallic wire-edged ribbon
- Spellbinders™ Nestabilities® die templates: Grand Labels Eleven (#LF-246), Lacey Ovals (#S4-314)
- Spellbinders™ Renaissance Hearts Pendants Shapeabilities® die templates (#S4-206)
- Spellbinders™ Grand Calibur® machine
- Paper piercer
- Double-sided tape
- Adhesive foam dots
- Paper adhesive

Candle Wrap

Project note: *Candle wrap is meant for decorative purposes only; if burning candle, please remove wrap. Never leave a burning candle unattended.*

Cut a piece of Curtain Call paper to fit around candle; wrap paper around candle and secure with double-sided tape on back.

Using #4 Grand Labels Eleven die template, die-cut and emboss a label from a 5 x 2½-inch piece of cream cardstock. Die-cut and emboss a #3 label from a 4½ x 2¼-inch piece of black cardstock. Die-cut and emboss a #2 label from a 4 x 1⅞-inch piece of gray/cream paper. Layer and adhere labels to candle as shown.

Using #2 Lacey Ovals die template, die-cut and emboss an oval from black cardstock.

Using Accent 2 Renaissance Hearts die template, die-cut and emboss an accent from gold metallic paper. Adhere to oval. Pierce a hole through center of layered die cuts; insert brad. Attach to candle using foam dots.

Wrap ribbon around candle. Tie bow and trim ends.

Sources: *Cardstock from WorldWin Papers; Curtain Call paper from Graphic 45; Willow papers from Anna Griffin Inc.; brad from Creative Impressions Inc.; die templates and die-cutting/embossing machine from Spellbinders™ Paper Arts; foam dots and paper adhesive from Helmar.*

Card Box

Project note: *When adhering paper to box, score edges to create clean folds.*

Cut box to desired size; cover with Curtain Call paper.

Referring to Selective Die Cutting technique and using #4 Grand Labels Eleven die template, die-cut and emboss a label from a 5 x 4-inch piece of cream cardstock. With short edge horizontal on work surface, score a horizontal line 1⅞ inches from curved edge of label. Referring to photo, adhere to box front, folding and adhering larger flap inside box.

In the same manner as before and using #3 Grand Labels Eleven die template, die-cut and emboss a label from a 5 x 2-inch piece of black cardstock. Die-cut and emboss a #2 label from a 4½ x 1¾-inch piece of gray/cream paper. Layer and adhere to box front as shown.

50TH ANNIVERSARY
You are invited to help us celebrate
the 50th anniversary of
Robert and Susan Smith.
When: Saturday. April 15th 7-9PM
Where: Centerville Community center
RSVP by April 1 by calling
(403) 443-0091

CARDS

GUEST BOOK

Using #2 Lacey Ovals die template, die-cut and emboss two ovals from black cardstock.

Using Accent 2 Renaissance Hearts Pendants die template, die-cut and emboss an accent from gold metallic paper. Adhere to a black oval. Pierce a hole through center of layered die cuts; insert brad. Attach to box as shown using foam dots.

Wrap ribbon around box; tie a bow, trim ends.

Hand-print or use a computer to generate "CARDS" onto cream cardstock. Referring to Die Cutting & Embossing Stamped Images technique and using #1 Classic Ovals LG die template, die-cut and emboss an oval around word. Adhere to remaining black oval. Place layered "CARDS" oval on top of a ribbon tail; pierce a hole through oval and ribbon tail. Insert brad, attaching oval to ribbon.

Cut a 1⅝ x 13-inch piece from black cardstock. Cut a 1⅜ x 13-inch piece from gray/cream paper; adhere to black cardstock piece. Adhere ends of layered piece inside box, forming a handle. Embellish with pearls.

Sources: *Cardstock from WorldWin Papers; Curtain Call paper from Graphic 45; Willow papers from Anna Griffin Inc.; brads from Creative Impressions Inc.; self-adhesive pearls from Want2Scrap; die templates and die-cutting/ embossing machine from Spellbinders™ Paper Arts; foam dots and paper adhesive from Helmar.*

Guest Book

Using #6 Grand Labels Eleven die template, die-cut and emboss a label from Curtain Call paper. Cut off top 2 inches; round top corners.

For front cover, die-cut and emboss a label from cream cardstock using #4 Grand Labels Eleven die template. With short edge horizontal on work surface, score a horizontal line 1½ inches below top edge. Fold flap down.

Using #3 Grand Labels Eleven die template, die-cut and emboss a label from black cardstock. Cut off 1¼ inches from top of black label. Adhere 1¼-inch piece to folded flap as shown. Adhere remaining piece of black label to main section of cream label, aligning straight edge with scored line.

Hand-print or use a computer to generate "GUEST BOOK" onto cream cardstock. Referring to Die Cutting & Embossing Stamped Images technique and using #2 Grand Labels Eleven die template, die-cut and emboss a label around words. Cut off ½ inch from top of label.

Materials

- Cardboard box
- Cardstock: cream, black
- Printed papers: Curtain Call, Willow gray/cream, Willow gold metallic
- Black fine-tip marker
- 2 small gold brads
- 5 small white self-adhesive pearls
- 27 inches 1-inch-wide gold metallic wire-edged ribbon
- Spellbinders™ Nestabilities® die templates: Grand Labels Eleven (#LF-246), Classic Ovals LG (#S4-110), Lacey Ovals (#S4-314)
- Spellbinders™ Renaissance Hearts Pendants Shapeabilities® die templates (#S4-206)
- Spellbinders™ Grand Calibur® machine
- Scoring tool
- Paper piercer
- Adhesive foam dots
- Repositionable tape
- Paper adhesive
- Computer with printer (optional)

Materials

- Cardstock: cream, black
- Printed papers: Curtain Call, Willow gray/cream, Willow gold metallic
- Vintage Banners stamp set
- Black chalk ink pad
- Black fine-tip marker
- Small gold brad
- Small white self-adhesive pearls
- Spellbinders™ Nestabilities® die templates: Grand Labels Eleven (#LF-246), Lacey Ovals (#S4-314)
- Spellbinders™ Renaissance Hearts Pendants Shapeabilities® die templates (#S4-206)
- Spellbinders™ Grand Calibur® machine
- Scoring tool
- Paper piercer
- Corner rounder
- Repositionable tape
- Paper adhesive
- Computer with printer (optional)

Referring to photo, adhere "GUEST BOOK" piece to black label aligning straight edge with scored line. Adhere flap in place.

Using #2 Grand Labels Eleven die template, die-cut and emboss a label from a 4½ x 1¼-inch piece of gray/cream paper. Adhere to folded flap; trim straight edge if needed before adhering.

Using #3 Grand Labels Eleven die template, die-cut and emboss several labels from cream cardstock, forming pages for guest book. Cut off 1 inch from top of each page. Stamp a flourish on bottom of each page, including "GUEST BOOK" cover page. Add a pearl to center of each flourish.

Using #2 Lacey Ovals die template, die-cut and emboss an oval from black cardstock.

Using Accent 2 Renaissance Hearts Pendants die template, die-cut and emboss an accent from gold metallic paper. Layer and adhere accent and oval die cuts to front cover page as shown.

Stack front cover, pages and Curtain Call label on top of each other as shown. Pierce a hole through center of accent die cut and pierce through all layers. Insert brad, securing layers together. Guest book will open by twisting cover to the side. ▪

Sources: *Cardstock from WorldWin Papers; Curtain Call paper from Graphic 45; Willow papers from Anna Griffin Inc.; stamp set from Waltzingmouse Stamps; chalk ink pad from Clearsnap Inc.; brads from Creative Impressions Inc.; self-adhesive pearls from Want2Scrap; die templates and die-cutting/embossing machine from Spellbinders™ Paper Arts; paper adhesive from Helmar.*

Did You Know?
You can use Spellbinders™ die templates with polymer clay and bake the clay in the die.

Ladies' Night Out

DESIGNS BY **LESLEY LANGDON**

Materials

- Felt: turquoise, red, yellow, pink
- Various sizes of black self-adhesive pearls
- Spellbinders™ Nestabilities® die templates: Classic Scalloped Circles LG (#S4-124), Classic Scalloped Circles SM (#S4-125)
- Spellbinders™ Grand Calibur® machine
- Hot-glue gun

Felt Flowers

Project notes: *If you have difficulty cutting felt with your die-cutting machine, try putting a piece of printer paper over the felt and die to get a cleaner cut. One #1 Classic Scalloped Circles SM (small) will be set aside for each flower. Some projects will use these extra scalloped circles, some will not.*

Using #1 Classic Scalloped Circles SM die template, die-cut two scalloped circles from desired color of felt; set one aside. Die-cut a #2 Classic Scalloped Circles SM from same-color felt.

In the same manner, using #1 Classic Scalloped Circles LG die template, die-cut a scalloped circle from same-color felt.

To create a flower, layer scalloped circles together and adhere using hot-glue; pinch top flower while glue is drying to create a textured look. Adhere various sizes of black pearls to center of flower.

Repeat process using different colors of felt as needed to complete each Card, Hair Clip, Plate Pin and Wineglass Marker.

Sources: *Self-adhesive pearls from Want2Scrap; die templates and die-cutting/embossing machine from Spellbinders™ Paper Arts; hot-glue gun from Glue Arts.*

Cards

Hand-print or use a computer to generate gift card sentiment onto cardstock as shown, leaving room to attach felt flower.

Referring to Die Cutting & Embossing Stamped Images technique and using #5 Curved Rectangles die template, die-cut and emboss a curved rectangle around words; do not remove die template. Referring to Using Die Templates as Stencils technique, ink edges of curved rectangle.

Hand-print or use a computer to generate "Welcome to LADIES nIgHt" onto cardstock. In the same manner as before and using #1 Grommet Tag die template, die-cut and emboss a tag around sentiment; ink tag. Attach tag to curved rectangle using foam squares as shown. Attach a pearl to each side of tag.

Following Felt Flowers instructions (above), create a flower and hot-glue it to center of card. Repeat for each card using a different-color felt flower for each.

Sources: *Distress ink pad from Ranger Industries Inc.; self-adhesive pearls from Want2Scrap; die templates and die-cutting/embossing machine from Spellbinders™ Paper Arts; hot-glue gun from Glue Arts; foam squares from SCRAPBOOK ADHESIVES BY 3L™.*

Materials

- White smooth cardstock
- Light brown distress ink pad
- Black fine-tip marker
- 2 large black self-adhesive pearls
- Spellbinders™ Curved Rectangles Nestabilities® die templates (#S5-006)
- Spellbinders™ Grommet Tags Shapeabilities® die templates (#S4-322)
- Spellbinders™ Grand Calibur® machine
- Craft sponge
- Hot-glue gun
- Adhesive foam squares
- Repositionable tape
- Paper adhesive
- Computer with printer (optional)

Did You Know?

Cutting 100% wool felt is as easy as cutting cardstock with Spellbinders™ dies and the Grand Calibur®.

Welcome to LADIES NIGHT

Welcome to LADIES NIGHT
Your col...

Welcome to LADIES NIGHT
Your color is YELLOW.

Welcome to LADIES NIGHT
...color is BLUE.

Welcome to LADIES NIGHT

Your color is PINK.

Put on your Hair Clip.
Tie on your Wine marker.
Pinch your Plate Pin.

and have fun.

Plate Pin

Hair Clip

Hair Clip

Hair Clip

Following Felt Flowers instructions (page 38), create a flower. **Note:** *The additional small die-cut scalloped circle will be used.* Using #5 Standard Circles SM die template, die-cut three circles from black netting. Fold each netting circle in half and hot-glue it to back of a felt flower, overlapping as desired.

Open a hair clip and place a small felt scalloped circle on inside of clip. Allow clip to close and place felt flower on top of clip, sandwiching clip between flower and small scalloped circle. Secure with hot glue. **Note:** *Do not get hot glue on inside of hair clip.*

Hand-print or use a computer to generate "Hair Clip" onto cardstock. In the same manner as for Card (page 38), use #2 Curved Rectangles die template to die-cut and emboss a curved rectangle around "Hair Clip" as shown; ink die cut. Attach hair clip to label.

Repeat for each hair clip using a different-color felt flower for each.

Sources: Distress ink pad from Ranger Industries Inc.; die templates and die-cutting/embossing machine from Spellbinders™ Paper Arts; hot-glue gun from Glue Arts.

Did You Know?

You can die-cut and layer fabrics, foils and felts to make your own embellishments for pillows, purses and other fun projects.

Plate Pin

Project note: *If black distressed clothespins are unavailable, color wooden clothespins with a black marker and distress using sandpaper.*

Following Felt Flowers instructions (page 38), create a flower. ***Note:*** *The additional small die-cut scalloped circle will be used.* Hot-glue felt flower to end of clothespin as shown; hot-glue small scalloped circle to reverse side of flower covering glue.

Hand-print or use a computer to generate "Plate Pin" onto cardstock. In the same manner as for Card (page 38), use #2 Curved Rectangles die template to

die-cut and emboss a curved rectangle around "Plate Pin"; ink die cut. Attach plate pin to label.

Repeat for each plate pin using a different-color felt flower for each.

Materials

- Black distressed clothespins
- White smooth cardstock
- Light brown distress ink pad
- Black fine-tip marker
- 2 large black self-adhesive pearls
- Spellbinders™ Curved Rectangles Nestabilities® die templates (#S5-006)
- Spellbinders™ Grand Calibur® machine
- Craft sponge
- Hot-glue gun
- Paper adhesive
- Computer with printer (optional)

Sources: *Clothespins from Canvas Corp; distress ink pad from Ranger Industries Inc.; die templates and die-cutting/embossing machine from Spellbinders™ Paper Arts; hot-glue gun from Glue Arts.*

Materials

- White smooth cardstock
- Light brown distress ink pad
- ½-inch-wide black decorative ribbon
- Black fine-tip marker
- Spellbinders™ Curved Rectangles Nestabilities® die templates (#S5-006)
- Spellbinders™ Grand Calibur® machine
- Craft sponge
- Hot-glue gun
- Paper adhesive
- Computer with printer (optional)

Wineglass Marker

Following Felt Flowers instructions (page 38), create a flower. ***Note:*** *The additional small die-cut scalloped circle will be used.* Cut a 24-inch length of ribbon.

Hot-glue felt flower to center of ribbon; hot-glue small scalloped circle to reverse side of ribbon covering hot glue.

Hand-print or use a computer to generate "Wine Marker" onto cardstock. In the same manner as for Card (page 38), use #2 Curved Rectangles die template to die-cut and emboss a curved rectangle around "Wine Marker" as shown; ink die cut. Wrap wineglass marker around label and tie a bow.

Repeat for each wineglass marker using a different-color felt flower for each. ■

Sources: *Distress ink pad from Ranger Industries Inc.; die templates and die-cutting/embossing machine from Spellbinders™ Paper Arts; hot-glue gun from Glue Arts.*

Happy Birthday

DESIGNS BY **TONYA DIRK**

Invitation

Form a 4¾ x 6¼-inch top-folded card from red cardstock. Referring to Selective Die Cutting technique and using #4 Scalloped Squares die template, die-cut bottom edge of card.

Using same die template, die-cut and emboss a scalloped square from black cardstock.

Trim scalloped square to a 4½ x 6-inch piece, leaving scalloped edges intact as shown. With long edge horizontal on work surface, score a vertical line ⅜ inch from left scalloped edge. Fold to front at scored line.

Hand-print using markers or use a computer to generate party invitation information as shown. Referring to Die Cutting & Embossing Stamped Images technique and using #4 Scalloped Squares die template, die-cut and emboss a scalloped square around text. Trim down to a 4⅜ x 5¾-inch piece, leaving bottom scalloped edge intact. Adhere to black piece as shown; fold and adhere flap on black piece to top of white piece. Adhere to card front.

Stamp pennants along bottom of white piece in rainbow colors. Using black ink, stamp dots between pennants.

Color gems with markers as shown; let dry. Attach gems to black dots.

Wrap baker's twine around top fold of card. Tie bow on left side; trim ends.

Sources: *Cardstock from Bazzill Basics Paper Inc.; stamp set from Gina K. Designs; pigment ink pads from Clearsnap Inc.; self-adhesive gems from Want2Scrap; die templates and die-cutting/embossing machine from Spellbinders™ Paper Arts; paper adhesive from SCRAPBOOK ADHESIVES BY 3L™.*

Materials

- Cardstock: red, white, black
- Perfect Pennants stamp set
- Pigment ink pads: orange, yellow, green, purple
- Chalk ink pads: red, blue, black
- Permanent markers: red, orange, yellow, green, blue, purple
- 7 small clear self-adhesive gems
- Red/white baker's twine
- Spellbinders™ Grand Scalloped Squares Nestabilities® die templates (#LF-127)
- Spellbinders™ Grand Calibur® machine
- Scoring tool
- Repositionable tape
- Paper adhesive
- Computer with color printer (optional)

You're Invited To A Party

For: Natasha's 6th Birthday

When: March 10th, 2012

Time: 12:00–4:00 p.m.

Where: Our House

Theme: Rainbows and Sunshine

CeLeBRaTe!
CeLeBRaTe!
CeLeBRaTe!
CeLeBRaTe!
CeLeBRaTe!
CeLeBRaTe!

You're my pot
of gold at the
end of the
RAINBOW

You're Invited To A Party

For: Natasha's 6th Birthday

When: March 10th, 2012

Time: 12:00-4:00 p.m.

Where: Our House

Theme: Rainbows and Sunshine

Materials

- Cardstock: red, orange, yellow, green, blue, purple, white, black
- Perfect Pennants stamp set
- Pigment ink pads: orange, yellow, green, purple
- Chalk ink pads: red, blue, black
- Permanent markers: red, orange, yellow, green, blue, purple
- 6 large clear self-adhesive gems
- Red/white baker's twine
- 2 wooden kabob sticks
- Spellbinders™ Shapeabilities® die templates: Nested Pennants (#S5-028), Nested Lacey Pennants (#S5-029)
- Spellbinders™ Grand Calibur® machine
- 1/16-inch hole punch
- Paper adhesive

Banner

Using #2 Nested Pennants die template, die-cut six pennants from white cardstock. Referring to photo, use different colors of ink to stamp a pennant on each white die-cut pennant.

Color gems with markers as shown; let dry. Attach gems to corresponding-color pennants.

Using #2 Nested Lacey Pennants die template, die-cut a lacey pennant from each of the following colors of cardstock: red, orange, yellow, green, blue and purple.

Adhere pennants and lacey pennants together as shown. Punch a 1/16-inch hole through both top corners of each layered pennant. Thread 34 inches of baker's twine through holes.

Using #3 ribbon Nested Lacey Pennants die template, die-cut five ribbons from black cardstock. Die-cut five ribbons from white cardstock with #2 ribbon Nested Lacey Pennants die template. Stamp "CeLeBraTe!" onto each white ribbon with black ink, reinking each time. Adhere white ribbons to black ribbons.

Adhere ribbons between pennants as shown.

Wrap one end of baker's twine around a kabob stick and tie a knot. Repeat with remaining end of twine.

Sources: *Cardstock from Bazzill Basics Paper Inc.; stamp set from Gina K. Designs; pigment ink pads from Clearsnap Inc.; self-adhesive gems from Want2Scrap; die templates and die-cutting/embossing machine from Spellbinders™ Paper Arts; paper adhesive from SCRAPBOOK ADHESIVES BY 3L™.*

Sucker Tag

Hand-print with black fine-tip and permanent markers, or use a computer to generate "You're my pot of gold at the end of the RAINBOW" as shown onto white cardstock. In the same manner as for Invitations (page 42) and using #2 Nested Pennants die template, die-cut a pennant around sentiment. Apply adhesive along edges of pennant; sprinkle with glitter. Let dry.

Using #2 Nested Lacey Pennants die template, die-cut a lacey pennant from red cardstock. Adhere pennants together.

Color gems with markers as shown; let dry. Attach gems to pennant.

Punch two $\frac{1}{16}$-inch holes through pennant as shown. Wrap baker's twine around sucker stick and tie a knot; thread ends of twine through pennant holes and tie a bow. Trim ends. ■

Sources: *Cardstock from Bazzill Basics Paper Inc.; self-adhesive gems from Want2Scrap; die templates and die-cutting/embossing machine from Spellbinders™ Paper Arts; paper adhesive from SCRAPBOOK ADHESIVES BY 3L™.*

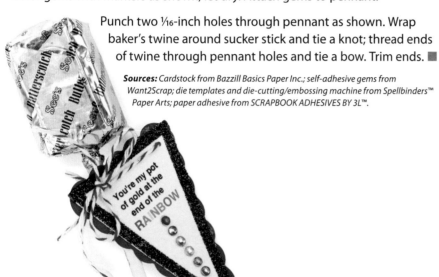

Materials

- Sucker
- Cardstock: red, white
- Black fine-tip marker
- Permanent markers: red, orange, yellow, green, blue, purple
- Black glitter
- 6 extra-small clear self-adhesive gems
- Red/white baker's twine
- Spellbinders™ Shapeabilities® die templates: Nested Pennants (#S5-028), Nested Lacey Pennants (#S5-029)
- Spellbinders™ Grand Calibur® machine
- $\frac{1}{16}$-inch hole punch
- Paper adhesive
- Computer with color printer (optional)

Did You Know?

You can use Nestabilities® die templates to cut windows in your card fronts. Add an embossed edge to create a beautiful frame.

Princess Party

DESIGNS BY **MICHELLE WOERNER**

Princess Tiara

Cut a ½-inch-wide strip of white cardstock long enough to fit around little girl's head. Adhere ends together forming a tiara base.

Using #7 and #3 Fleur de Lis Accents die templates, die-cut and emboss a border and an accent piece from pink glitter cardstock. Trim border down to a 7½-inch length. Adhere to front of tiara base. Embellish border with five yellow gems. Place remaining gem on accent piece as shown.

Using #5 Blossom die template, die-cut and emboss a blossom from printed paper. Cut off ⅝ inch from bottom edge of blossom.

Hand-print or use a computer to generate little girl's name onto white cardstock. Referring to Die Cutting & Embossing Stamped Images technique and using #2 Standard Circles SM die template, die-cut and emboss a circle around name. Attach pink circle frame around outer edge of circle.

Adhere name circle and pink glitter accent to die-cut blossom shape as shown. Referring to photo, adhere to inside edge of tiara base.

Sources: *Cardstock from Gina K. Designs and Best Creations Inc.; printed paper from Echo Park Paper Co.; self-adhesive gems from Want2Scrap; die templates and die-cutting/embossing machine from Spellbinders™ Paper Arts; paper adhesive from Tombow USA.*

Materials

- Cardstock: white, pink glitter
- Little Girl Blush/Leaf printed paper
- Black marker
- Self-adhesive gems: 6 medium-size yellow, 1 pink circle frame
- Spellbinders™ Nestabilities® die templates: Standard Circles SM (#S4-116), Blossom (#S4-192)
- Spellbinders™ Shapeabilities® Fleur de Lis Accents (#S5-042)
- Spellbinders™ Grand Calibur® machine
- Repositionable tape
- Paper adhesive

Emma

Sweet princess

Materials

- Cardstock: white, pink, pink glitter
- My Little Princess stamp set
- Black dye ink pad
- Copic® markers: R39, RV29, RV42, Y02
- Silver tinsel strands
- 3½-inch wooden craft picks
- Spellbinders™ Nestabilities® die templates: Standard Circles SM (#S4-116), Stars Five (#S4-092)
- Spellbinders™ Grand Calibur® machine
- Yellow glitter glue
- Adhesive foam squares
- Repositionable tape
- Paper adhesive

Magic Wands

Using #3 Stars Five die template, die-cut and emboss one base star from colored cardstock. If desired, decorate base star with markers and glitter.

Stamp desired image onto white cardstock. Color using markers. In the same manner as for Princess Tiara (page 46) and using #2 Standard Circles SM or #2 Stars Five die template, die-cut and emboss shape around image. Color edges yellow with marker as desired.

Attach stamped image to base star using foam squares. Tie a tinsel strand around craft pick. Attach craft pick to back of star with a foam square.

Sources: *Cardstock from Gina K. Designs and Best Creations Inc.; stamp set from Technique Tuesday; markers from Imagination International Inc.; die templates and die-cutting/embossing machine from Spellbinders™ Paper Arts; glitter glue from Ranger Industries Inc.; foam squares from SCRAPBOOK ADHESIVES BY 3L™; paper adhesive from Tombow USA.*

Invitation

Using #6 Classic Scalloped Squares LG die template, die-cut and emboss two scalloped squares from Blush/Leaf paper. On one scalloped square, score a horizontal line ½ inch below top edge. Adhere to un-scored square, applying adhesive to ½-inch flap only and forming a 4 x 4-inch top-folded card.

Stamp princess and "Sweet princess" onto white cardstock. Color using markers. In the same manner as for Princess Tiara (page 46) and using #7 Classic Squares LG die template, die-cut and emboss a square around stamped images.

Cut a 3½ x ¼-inch piece from pink glitter cardstock and a 3½ x ⅝-inch piece from Jody's Stripe paper. Layer and adhere pieces to bottom of image square as shown.

Wrap twine twice around square and tie a bow on left side; trim ends. Adhere to card front. Embellish bow with rhinestone.

Hand-print or use a computer to generate invitation information onto white cardstock. Stamp birds on either side of text; color using markers. In the same manner as before and using #7 Classic Squares die template, die-cut and emboss a square around text.

Cut a 3½ x ¼-inch piece from pink glitter cardstock and a 3½ x ½-inch piece from Jody's Stripe paper. Layer and adhere pieces to bottom of square as shown. Adhere inside card.

Sources: Cardstock from Gina K. Designs and Best Creations Inc.; printed paper from Echo Park Paper Co.; stamp set from Technique Tuesday; markers from Imagination International Inc.; self-adhesive gem from Want2Scrap; die templates and die-cutting/embossing machine from Spellbinders™ Paper Arts; paper adhesive from Tombow USA.

Materials

- Cardstock: white, pink glitter
- Little Girl printed papers: Jody's Stripe, Blush/Leaf
- My Little Princess stamp set
- Black dye ink pad
- Black fine-tip marker
- Copic markers: E00, E25, E33, R000, R21, RV29, RV42, RV55, Y11, Y15
- Pink self-adhesive rhinestone
- Pink/white baker's twine
- Spellbinders™ Nestabilities® die templates: Classic Squares LG (#S4-126), Classic Scalloped Squares LG (#S4-127)
- Spellbinders™ Grand Calibur® machine
- Scoring tool
- Repositionable tape
- Paper adhesive
- Computer with printer (optional)

Materials

- Flat-bottom glassine bag
- Cardstock: white, pink glitter
- Little Girl Chloe Crowns printed paper
- My Little Princess stamp set
- Black dye ink pad
- Copic markers: R39, RV29, RV42, Y02
- 9 inches ⅜-inch-wide pink satin-edged sheer ribbon
- Candy
- Spellbinders™ Nestabilities® die templates: Standard Circles SM (#S4-116), Blossom (#S4-192)
- Spellbinders™ Grand Calibur® machine
- ⅛-inch hole punch
- Scoring tool
- Yellow glitter glue
- Adhesive foam squares
- Repositionable tape
- Paper adhesive

Treat Bag

Cut a 2½ x 2½-inch piece from printed paper. Score a line down center of piece and fold in half.

Fill bag with candy. Place folded-paper piece over top of bag. Punch two ⅛-inch holes through top of bag as shown. Thread ribbon through holes; tie bow on front and trim ends.

Stamp crown onto white cardstock and color using markers; apply glitter glue to hearts, let dry. In the same manner as for Princess Tiara and using #2 Standard Circles SM die template, die-cut and emboss a circle around stamped image.

Using #2 Blossom die template, die-cut and emboss a blossom from pink glitter cardstock. Layer and adhere die-cut pieces to bag as shown, using foam squares. ■

Sources: Cardstock from Gina K. Designs and Best Creations Inc.; printed paper from Echo Park Paper Co.; stamp set from Technique Tuesday; markers from Imagination International Inc.; die templates and die-cutting/embossing machine from Spellbinders™ Paper Arts; glitter glue from Ranger Industries Inc.; foam squares from SCRAPBOOK ADHESIVES BY 3L™; paper adhesive from Tombow USA.

Stars Graduation Set

DESIGNS BY **JUDY HAYES**

Invitation

Cut a 3⅝ x 8½-inch piece from white cardstock to form invitation base. Cut a 3¼ x 8-inch piece from printed paper. Adhere to red cardstock; trim a small border. Adhere to invitation base.

Hand-print or use a computer to generate party information onto text-weight paper. Cut a 2⅞ x 5¼-inch rectangle around party information. Adhere to invitation as shown.

Using #1 Stars Five die template, die-cut and emboss one star from red cardstock. Die-cut and emboss two stars from red cardstock using #3 Stars Five die template.

Referring to Making Frames technique and using #4 and #2 Stars Five die templates, die-cut and emboss a star frame from silver cardstock. Adhere one large red star to back of star frame, covering opening.

Adhere stars to invitation using foam squares as desired.

Sources: White and red cardstock from Bazzill Basics Paper Inc.; silver Mirricard cardstock from The Paper Cut; printed paper from Scrapbook Customs; die templates and die-cutting/embossing machine from Spellbinders™ Paper Arts; adhesive foam squares and paper adhesive from SCRAPBOOK ADHESIVES BY 3L™.

Materials

- Cardstock: white, red, silver Mirricard
- White text-weight paper
- Graduation Mini Words printed paper
- Black fine-tip marker
- Spellbinders™ Stars Five Nestabilities® die templates (#S4-092)
- Spellbinders™ Grand Calibur® machine
- Adhesive foam squares
- Repositionable tape
- Paper adhesive
- Computer with printer (optional)

Materials

- 4 x 4 x 4-inch white gift box
- Cardstock: red, silver Mirricard
- Graduation Mini Words printed paper
- 13 inches silver cord
- Spellbinders™ Nestabilities® die templates: Stars Five (#S4-092), Classic Squares LG (#S4-126)
- Spellbinders™ Grand Calibur® machine
- Adhesive foam squares
- Repositionable tape
- Paper adhesive

Gift Box

Using #7 Classic Squares LG die template, die-cut and emboss five squares from printed paper. Adhere to box as shown.

In the same manner as for Invitation (above) and using #4 and #2 Stars Five die templates, die-cut and emboss five star frames from silver cardstock. ***Note:*** *Set aside center star cutouts as they will be used later.*

Using #3 Stars Five die template, die-cut and emboss five stars from red cardstock. Adhere a red star to back of each star frame covering openings. Adhere four star frames to sides of box as shown.

Adhere two silver center star cutouts together, sandwiching one end of silver cord between stars. Repeat with two more center star cutouts at opposite end of cord.

Using #1 Stars Five die template, die-cut and emboss four stars from red cardstock. Adhere red stars to silver stars at ends of cord.

Loop cord and adhere to center top of box. Adhere remaining star frame to box lid. Using #2 Stars Five die template, die-cut and emboss a star from red cardstock. Attach to box lid using a foam square.

Sources: Gift box from Oriental Trading Co.; red cardstock from Bazzill Basics Paper Inc.; silver Mirricard cardstock from The Paper Cut; printed paper from Scrapbook Customs; die templates and die-cutting/embossing machine from Spellbinders™ Paper Arts; adhesive foam squares and paper adhesive from SCRAPBOOK ADHESIVES BY 3L™.

Congratulations
you've done it!

You're invited to

David's Graduation Party

Please join us
as we celebrate
David's graduation
from
Red Rock High School

Saturday, May 26, 2012
2:00-5:00 pm

Prairie Community Center
630 Main St
St. Joseph, Minnesota

RSVP to Lisa
lisa@gmail.com or 506-622-1321
by April 30th

Table Topper

Using #4 Pennant Nested Pennants die template, die-cut and emboss two pennants from white cardstock and two pennants from printed paper. Cut bottom ½ inch off wide end of both printed paper pennants. Adhere printed paper pennants to white pennants. Adhere pennants together applying adhesive to top 1½-inch section only.

Using #4 Labels Twenty-One die template, die-cut and emboss a label from white cardstock. With long edge horizontal on work surface, score vertical lines 1⅜ inches, 2¼ inches and 3⅛ inches from left edge. Beginning with a valley fold, accordion-fold along scored lines. Adhere side flaps of folded label to reverse sides of white pennants along bottom edge, forming a base for table topper.

Stamp congratulations sentiment onto white cardstock. Sprinkle with embossing powder; heat-emboss.

Referring to Die Cutting & Embossing Stamped Images technique and using #2 Ribbon Tags Trio Two die template, die-cut and emboss a tag around sentiment. Cut off right edge of tag and round edges.

Using #1 ribbon Nested Pennants die template, die-cut and emboss one ribbon each from red and silver cardstock. Adhere ribbons to back right edge of sentiment tag. Attach to table topper base using foam squares.

In the same manner as for Invitation (page 50) and using #5 and #3 Stars Five die templates, die-cut and emboss two star frames from silver cardstock. **Note:** *Set aside center star cutouts as they will be used later.*

Using #4 Stars Five die template, die-cut and emboss two stars from red cardstock. Adhere red stars to backs of star frames, covering openings. Adhere star frames to top of table topper base as shown, sandwiching top of base between frames.

Using #3 Stars Five die template, die-cut and emboss a star from red cardstock. In the same manner, die-cut and emboss two #2 stars from silver cardstock and one star from red cardstock. Die-cut and emboss two #1 stars from red cardstock.

Layer and adhere stars to table topper as desired, using foam squares as desired. ■

Sources: *White and red cardstock from Bazzill Basics Paper Inc.; silver Mirricard from The Paper Cut; printed paper from Scrapbook Customs; stamp from Penny Black Inc.; fine-detail ink pad from Tsukineko LLC; embossing powder from Ranger Industries Inc.; die templates and die-cutting/embossing machine from Spellbinders™ Paper Arts; adhesive foam squares and paper adhesive from SCRAPBOOK ADHESIVES BY 3L™.*

Halloween Party

DESIGNS BY **AJ OTTO**

Place Card

Using #5 Long Classic Scalloped Rectangles LG die template, die-cut and emboss a scalloped rectangle from black cardstock. With long edge horizontal on work surface, score a vertical line 3⅛ inches from left edge. Fold at scored line, forming a 3⅛ x 3⅛-inch top-folded card.

Using #5 Classic Squares LG die template, die-cut and emboss a square from printed paper. Adhere to card front.

Using #3 Labels Eighteen die template, die-cut and emboss a label from white cardstock.

Attach stickers to label to spell out desired name. Stamp a bat and jack-o'-lanterns on label as shown. Adhere label to card front.

Sources: Cardstock and stamp set from Gina K. Designs; printed paper from My Mind's Eye; alphabet stickers from American Crafts Inc.; die templates and die-cutting/embossing machine from Spellbinders™ Paper Arts; paper adhesive from SCRAPBOOK ADHESIVES BY 3L™.

Materials

- Cardstock: black, white
- Black Bird Big Dots printed paper
- Alphabet stickers
- Boo! stamp set
- Dye ink pads: black, orange
- Spellbinders™ Nestabilities® die templates: Long Classic Scalloped Rectangles LG (#S4-143), Classic Squares LG (#S4-126), Labels Eighteen (#S4-310)
- Spellbinders™ Grand Calibur® machine
- Scoring tool
- Paper adhesive

Materials

- Small kraft-paper bag
- Cardstock: black, white
- Black Bird Big Dots printed paper
- Stamp sets: Garden Silhouettes, Lovely Labels 3
- Dye ink pads: black, orange
- 11 inches ⅜-inch-wide olive green/white stitched ribbon
- White thread
- Spellbinders™ Nestabilities® die templates: Long Classic Scalloped Rectangles LG (#S4-143), Long Classic Rectangles LG (#S4-142), Labels Eighteen (#S4-310), Standard Circles SM (#S4-116), Standard Circles LG (#S4-114)
- Spellbinders™ Grand Calibur® machine
- Adhesive foam squares
- Repositionable tape
- Paper adhesive

Snack Sack

Wrap ribbon around paper sack, allowing ends to extend past left edge. Tie thread around ribbon ends and knot; trim ends long.

Using #4 Long Classic Scalloped Rectangles LG die template, die-cut and emboss a scalloped rectangle from black cardstock. Die-cut and emboss a rectangle from printed paper using #4 Long Classic Rectangles LG die template. Layer and adhere rectangles to sack.

Using #4 Labels Eighteen die template, die-cut and emboss a label from white cardstock. Stamp diamond background onto label with orange ink. Attach to sack as shown using foam squares.

Stamp "FOR YOU" onto white cardstock with black ink. Referring to Die Cutting & Embossing Stamped Images technique and using #2 Standard Circles LG die template, die-cut and emboss a circle around sentiment.

Die-cut and emboss a circle from black cardstock using #3 Standard Circles SM die template. Adhere circles together. Adhere to label with foam squares.

Sources: Cardstock and stamp sets from Gina K. Designs; printed paper from My Mind's Eye; die templates and die-cutting/embossing machine from Spellbinders™ Paper Arts; foam squares and paper adhesive from SCRAPBOOK ADHESIVES BY 3L™.

Materials

- Cardstock: orange, white
- Black Bird Big Dots printed paper
- Black alphabet stickers
- 28 inches ¾-inch-wide black/white decorative ribbon
- Spellbinders™ Nestabilities® die templates: Large Labels (#S4-168), Labels Eighteen (#S4-310)
- Spellbinders™ Grand Calibur® machine
- Adhesive foam squares
- Paper adhesive

Banner

Using #4 Large Labels die template, die-cut and emboss three labels from orange cardstock.

Using #3 Labels Eighteen die template, die-cut and emboss three labels from printed paper. Die-cut and emboss three labels from white cardstock using #2 Labels Eighteen die template. Layer and adhere labels to orange labels with foam squares.

Attach stickers to labels as shown to spell "boo."

Center and adhere labels to ribbon as shown. Tie a knot on each end of ribbon.

Sources: Cardstock from Gina K. Designs and Stampin' Up!; printed paper from My Mind's Eye; letter stickers from American Crafts Inc.; die templates and die-cutting/embossing machine from Spellbinders™ Paper Arts; foam squares and paper adhesive from SCRAPBOOK ADHESIVES BY 3L™.

Luminary

Project note: Do not place a burning candle inside luminary; use only battery-powered tea lights.

Cut a 10½ x 4¼-inch piece from orange cardstock. With long edge horizontal on work surface, score vertical lines 2½ inches, 5 inches, 7½ inches and 10 inches from left edge.

Referring to Making Windows technique and using #3 Standard Circles SM die template, die-cut a window centered on each 2½-inch-wide section of orange piece ⅞ inch below top edge.

Referring to Making Frames technique and using #2 Classic Scalloped Circles LG and #3 Standard Circles SM die templates, die-cut and emboss four frames from printed paper. Attach a frame over each circle window with foam squares.

Cut four 2 x 2¼-inch pieces from vellum. Stamp bats on each vellum piece with black ink. Adhere vellum pieces behind circle windows.

Fold orange piece at scored lines to form luminary and secure by adhering ½-inch flap to inside edge. ▪

Materials

- Orange cardstock
- Vellum
- Black Bird Big Dots printed paper
- Boo! stamp set
- Black dye ink pad
- Spellbinders™ Nestabilities® die templates: Standard Circles SM (#S4-116), Classic Scalloped Circles LG (#S4-124)
- Spellbinders™ Grand Calibur® machine
- Scoring tool
- Adhesive foam squares
- Repositionable tape
- Paper adhesive

Sources: Cardstock from Stampin' Up!; stamp set from Gina K. Designs; printed paper from My Mind's Eye; die templates and die-cutting/embossing machine from Spellbinders™ Paper Arts; foam squares and paper adhesive from SCRAPBOOK ADHESIVES BY 3L™.

Did You Know?

Stamps are available that coordinate perfectly with these die templates making it easy to stamp, cut, emboss and stencil for the ultimate layered effect.

Holiday Dinner

DESIGNS BY **GINA KRUPSKY**

Wineglass Decoration

Project note: *Try making wineglass decorations in different colors so guests can tell which wineglass is theirs.*

Using Accent 1 2010 Snowflake Pendants die template, die-cut and emboss a

snowflake from cardstock; remove center of die cut. Color snowflake using glitter pen as desired.

Cut a diagonal slit through one side of snowflake. Gently open at slit and slide onto stem of wineglass.

Materials

- White pearlescent cardstock
- Gold glitter gel pen
- Spellbinders™ 2010 Snowflake Pendants Shapeabilities® die templates (#S4-286)
- Spellbinders™ Grand Calibur® machine

Sources: *Cardstock from Gina K. Designs; glitter gel pen from Sakura of America; die templates and die-cutting/embossing machine from Spellbinders™ Paper Arts.*

Materials

- White pearlescent cardstock
- Gold glitter gel pen
- Small red button
- Small white brad
- 8 inches ⅝-inch-wide red/gold decorative ribbon
- Spellbinders™ Shapeabilities® die templates: 2010 Snowflake Pendants (#S4-286), Fleur de Lis Pendants (#S4-204)
- Spellbinders™ Grand Calibur® machine
- Paper piercer
- Adhesive foam dots
- Adhesive dots
- Paper adhesive

Candle Wrap

Project note: *For decorative purposes only; never leave a burning candle unattended.*

Using Accent 1 snowflake die template, die-cut and emboss a snowflake from cardstock. Color snowflake using glitter pen as desired.

Using center Fleur de Lis Pendants die template, die-cut and emboss a center from cardstock.

Attach snowflake to center die cut with foam dots. Adhere button to center of die cuts.

Cut ends of ribbon at an angle. Referring to photo, create a loop with ribbon. Pierce a hole through ribbon where it crisscrosses over itself; insert brad. Using an adhesive dot, attach layered die cuts to brad.

Sources: *Cardstock, button and ribbon from Gina K. Designs; glitter gel pen from Sakura of America; die templates and die-cutting/embossing machine from Spellbinders™ Paper Arts; foam dots from Plaid Enterprises Inc./All Night Media; adhesive dots from Glue Dots; paper adhesive from Tombow USA.*

Did You Know?
You can cut shrink art with Spellbinders™ dies?

Materials

- White pearlescent cardstock
- Gold glitter gel pen
- Large red button
- Small white brad
- 10 inches ⅝-inch-wide red/gold decorative ribbon
- Spellbinders™ 2010 Snowflake Pendants Shapeabilities® die templates (#S4-286)
- Spellbinders™ Grand Calibur® machine
- Paper piercer
- Adhesive foam dots
- Adhesive dots
- Paper adhesive

Napkin Wrap

Using 2010 Snowflake Pendants die template, die-cut and emboss pendant snowflake from cardstock. In the same manner, die-cut and emboss Accent 1 snowflake from cardstock. Color both snowflakes using glitter pen as desired.

Attach small snowflake to large snowflake with foam dots. Adhere button to small snowflake.

Cut ends of ribbon at an angle. Create a 2-inch-diameter loop with ribbon. Pierce a hole through ribbon where it crisscrosses over itself; insert brad. Using an adhesive dot, attach layered die cuts to brad.

Sources: *Cardstock, button and ribbon from Gina K. Designs; glitter gel pen from Sakura of America; die templates and die-cutting/embossing machine from Spellbinders™ Paper Arts; foam dots from Plaid Enterprises Inc./All Night Media; adhesive dots from Glue Dots; paper adhesive from Tombow USA.*

Place Card

Stamp label and desired name or sentiment onto white cardstock as shown. Referring to Die Cutting & Embossing Stamped Images technique and using #3 Labels Fourteen die template, die-cut and emboss a label around stamped label. Die-cut a matching label from white cardstock.

With long edge of unstamped label horizontal on work surface, score a horizontal line ¼ inch below top edge. Adhere ¼-inch flap to back of stamped die-cut label, creating a place card with a stand.

Materials

- White cardstock
- Jovial Pomegranate printed paper
- Stamp sets: Notes to Mom, Labeled With Love
- Black dye ink pad
- Gold glitter gel pen
- Spellbinders™ Labels Fourteen Nestabilities® die templates (#S4-290)
- Spellbinders™ Grand Calibur® machine
- Craft knife
- Repositionable tape
- Paper adhesive

Stamp label onto printed paper; cut out. Using a craft knife, cut out center oval of label. Adhere label to front of place card as shown. Embellish with glitter pen as desired.

Sources: Cardstock and stamp sets from Gina K. Designs; printed paper from BasicGrey; glitter gel pen from Sakura of America; die templates and die-cutting/embossing machine from Spellbinders™ Paper Arts; paper adhesive from Tombow USA and Sakura of America.

Menu

Hand-print or use a computer to generate menu information onto white matte cardstock. Trim down to a 5 x 7¾-inch panel. Adhere to green cardstock; trim a small border.

Wrap ribbon vertically along left edge of menu as shown; secure ends to back. Center and adhere to a 5½ x 8¼-inch piece of red cardstock.

Using 2010 Snowflake Pendants die template, die-cut and emboss pendant snowflake from white pearlescent cardstock. In the same manner, die-cut and emboss Accent 1 snowflake from white pearlescent cardstock. Color both snowflakes using glitter pen as desired.

Using foam dots, attach snowflakes together. Adhere button to center of small snowflake. Attach to upper left corner of menu. ■

Sources: Cardstock, button and ribbon from Gina K. Designs; glitter gel pen from Sakura of America; die templates and die-cutting/embossing machine from Spellbinders™ Paper Arts; foam dots from Plaid Enterprises Inc./All Night Media; paper adhesive from Tombow USA.

Materials

- Cardstock: red, green, white pearlescent, white matte
- Gold glitter gel pen
- Black fine-tip marker
- Medium red button
- 10 inches ⅜-inch-wide red/white polka-dot ribbon
- Spellbinders™ 2010 Snowflake Pendants Shapeabilities® die templates (#S4-286)
- Spellbinders™ Grand Calibur® machine
- Paper piercer
- Adhesive foam dots
- Paper adhesive
- Computer with printer (optional)

Did You Know?

You can use your die templates to cut photos along with cardstock, making it easy to have perfect mats each and every time.

New Year's Party

DESIGNS BY **JUDY HAYES**

Coasters

Project note: *Apply adhesive sheet to back side of each piece of cardstock or printed paper before die-cutting. If coaster has a plastic coating, peel off coating before adhering die-cut pieces.*

Using #7 Classic Squares LG die template, die-cut a square from Ornamental paper. Peel off adhesive backing and adhere to top of coaster.

Stamp desired circle sentiment onto Candy Canes paper as shown. Sprinkle with embossing powder; heat-emboss. Color holly using markers. Referring to Die Cutting & Embossing Stamped Images and Making Frames techniques, and using #4 and #6 Standard Circles LG die templates, die-cut a ring around sentiment. In the same manner as before, adhere to coaster.

Using #4 Standard Circle LG die template, die-cut a circle from Old St. Nick paper. Adhere to coaster.

To make coaster waterproof, spray a thin coating of decoupage medium onto coaster; let dry completely.

Repeat for remaining coasters.

Sources: *Cardstock from Bazzill Basics Paper Inc.; printed papers from My Mind's Eye; stamp set from JustRite Stampers®; markers from Imagination International Inc.; die templates and die-cutting/embossing machine from Spellbinders™ Paper Arts; adhesive sheet and paper adhesive from SCRAPBOOK ADHESIVES BY 3L™.*

Materials

- 3½ x 3½-inch cork coaster
- Red cardstock
- Holly Jolly printed papers: Ornamental, Old St. Nick, Candy Canes
- Christmas Ornament 3¼-inch stamp set (#JB-09790)
- Black pigment ink pad
- Clear embossing powder
- Copic® markers: G29, R39
- Spellbinders™ Nestabilities® die templates: Classic Squares LG (#S4-126), Standard Circles LG (#S4-114)
- Spellbinders™ Grand Calibur® machine
- Embossing heat tool
- Matte decoupage medium spray
- Adhesive sheet
- Repositionable tape
- Paper adhesive

Materials

- Red cardstock
- Holly Jolly printed papers: Ornamental, Old St. Nick, Candy Canes
- Merry Little Christmas stamp set (#JB-08780)
- Black pigment ink pad
- Clear embossing powder
- Copic markers: G29, R39
- Black fine-tip marker
- Extra-small gold jingle bells
- Red/white baker's twine
- ¹⁄₁₆-inch hole punch
- Spellbinders™ Nestabilities® die templates: Standard Circles LG (#S4-114), Standard Circles SM (#S4-116)
- Spellbinders™ Grand Calibur® machine
- Embossing heat tool
- Adhesive sheet
- Repositionable tape
- Paper adhesive

Wineglass Markers

Project note: *Apply adhesive sheet to back side of each piece of printed paper before die-cutting.*

Using #3 Standard Circles LG die template, die-cut a circle from red cardstock.

Using #3 Standard Circles SM die template, die-cut a circle from Old St. Nick paper. Peel off adhesive sheet backing and adhere to red circle.

Stamp holly circle onto Candy Cane paper as shown. Sprinkle with embossing powder; heat-emboss. Color holly using markers. In the same manner as for Coaster (above) and using #2 and #3 Standard Circles SM die templates, die-cut a ring around holly. Adhere to layered circle as shown.

Using #1 Standard Circles SM die template, die-cut and emboss a circle opening from center of layered circles, setting center circle cutout aside.

Die-cut and emboss a #1 Standard Circles SM circle from Candy Cane paper. Adhere small circle to solid red side of center circle cutout.

Using fine-tip marker, hand-print guest's name onto light-color side of small circle. Punch a ¹⁄₁₆-inch hole through top center of circle.

Celebrate the joys of Friendship
and the warmth of the season!

Please join us
in
Celebration of the New Year
December 31, 2011
7:00 p.m.
Our home

Dennis & Judy

Did You Know?
You can lay the entire package of circle Nestabilities® on your mat and cut them all out at once to create stacking rings. Try this with other shapes too!

Punch a 1/16-inch hole 1/8 inch from outside edge of wineglass marker. Thread twine through hole on wineglass marker; slide on a jingle bell and then thread through hole on name tag circle. Tie a bow and trim ends.

Directly across from attached name tag, cut wineglass marker from edge to center to allow placement around wineglass stem.

Repeat for remaining wineglass markers.

Sources: Cardstock from Bazzill Basics Paper Inc.; printed papers from My Mind's Eye; stamp set from JustRite Stampers®; pigment ink pad from Tsukineko LLC; markers from Imagination International Inc.; die templates and die-cutting/embossing machine from Spellbinders™ Paper Arts; adhesive sheet and paper adhesive from SCRAPBOOK ADHESIVES BY 3L™.

Invitations

Project note: *Apply adhesive sheet to Candy Canes paper before die-cutting.*

Cut a 4 x 4⅝-inch invitation base from red cardstock. Cut a 3¾ x 1¾-inch piece from Ornamental paper. Adhere to invitation base as shown.

Hand-print or use a computer to generate invitation information onto white cardstock. Trim down to a 3⅝ x 2⅝-inch piece; adhere to invitation base as shown.

Wrap twine around invitation; tie bow on left side and trim ends.

In the same manner as for Coaster (page 60) and using #4 and #7 Standard Circles SM die templates, die-cut a ring from red cardstock.

Stamp desired circle sentiment onto Candy Canes paper as shown. Sprinkle with embossing powder; heat-emboss. Color holly using markers. In the same manner as for Coaster and using #4 and #6 Standard Circles LG die templates, die-cut and emboss a ring around sentiment. Peel off adhesive backing and adhere to red ring.

Using #4 Standard Circles LG die template, die-cut a circle from Old St. Nick paper. Adhere to back of layered ring. Adhere to invitation base as shown.

Repeat for remaining invitations. ■

Sources: Cardstock from Bazzill Basics Paper Inc.; printed papers from My Mind's Eye; stamp set from JustRite Stampers®; markers from Imagination International Inc.; die templates and die-cutting/embossing machine from Spellbinders™ Paper Arts; adhesive sheet and paper adhesive from SCRAPBOOK ADHESIVES BY 3L™.

Materials

- Cardstock: red, white smooth
- Holly Jolly printed papers: Ornamental, Old St. Nick, Candy Canes
- Christmas Ornament 3¼-inch stamp set (#JB-09790)
- Black pigment ink pad
- Clear embossing powder
- Copic markers: G29, R39
- Black fine-tip marker
- Red/white baker's twine
- Spellbinders™ Nestabilities® die templates: Standard Circles LG (#S4-114), Standard Circles SM (#S4-116)
- Spellbinders™ Grand Calibur® machine
- Embossing heat tool
- Adhesive sheet
- Repositionable tape
- Paper adhesive
- Computer with printer (optional)

Easter Party

CONTINUED FROM PAGE 12

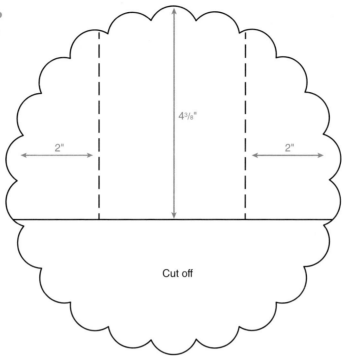

Easter Party Place Card Pocket
Cut along solid line; score along dashed lines

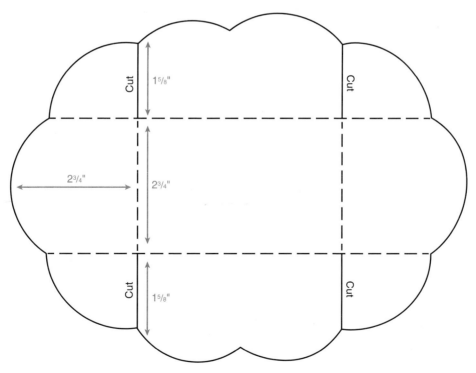

Easter Party Basket
Cut along solid lines; score along dashed lines

DESIGNERS

Stacey Caron
http://spellbinderspaperarts.com/
community/blog.aspx

Kazan Clark
www.nunutoolies.blogspot.com

Kimberly Crawford
www.kimberly-crawford.blogspot.com

Tonya Dirk
http://creativit-tonya.blogspot.com/

Becca Feeken
www.amazingpapergrace.com

Judy Hayes
www.judyhayesdesign.blogspot.com

Gina Krupsky
www.stamptv.ning.com

Lesley Langdon
http://lesleylangdoncreative.
blogspot.com/

Tina McDonald
http://tinamcd-mysanity.blogspot.com/

AJ Otto
http://thewillowgarden.blogspot.com/

Julie Overby
www.joverby.blogspot.com

Mona Pendleton
http://cupcakescreations.blogspot.com/

Karen Taylor
http://creativeyearnings.blogspot.com/

Michelle Woerner
http://stopandstamptheroses.
blogspot.com/

Latisha Yoast
http://crafteebee.blogspot.com/

BUYER'S GUIDE

Advantus Corp./The Girls' Paperie
(904) 482-0091
www.thegirlspaperie.com

American Crafts Inc.
(801) 226-0747
www.americancrafts.com

Anna Griffin Inc.
(888) 817-8170
www.annagriffin.com

BasicGrey
(801) 544-1116
www.basicgrey.com

Bazzill Basics Paper Inc.
(800) 560-1610
www.bazzillbasics.com

Beacon Adhesives Inc.
(914) 699-3405
www.beaconcreates.com

Best Creations Inc.
www.bestcreation.us

Canvas Corp.
(866) 376-9961
www.canvascorp.com

Clearsnap Inc.
(800) 448-4862
www.clearsnap.com

Core'dinations
www.coredinations.com

Cosmo Cricket
(800) 852-8810
www.cosmocricket.com

Creative Impressions Inc.
(719) 596-4860
www.creativeimpressions.com

Donna Salazar Designs
www.donnasalazar.com

Echo Park Paper Co.
(800) 701-1115
www.echoparkpaper.com

Flourishes
(888) 475-1575
www.flourishes.org

Gina K. Designs
(608) 838-3258
www.ginakdesigns.com

Glue Arts
(866) 889-4583
www.gluearts.com

Glue Dots
(888) 458-3368
www.gluedots.com

Graphic 45
(866) 573-4806
www.g45papers.com

Helmar
www.helmarusa.typepad.com

Imagination International Inc.
(541) 684-0013
www.copicmarker.com

JustRite Stampers®
(866) 405-6414
www.JustRite
Stampers®stampers.com

Lawn Fawn
www.lawnfawn.com

My Mind's Eye
(800) 665-5116
www.mymindseye.com

Oriental Trading Co.
(800) 348-6483
www.orientaltrading.com

The Paper Cut
(920) 954-6210
www.thepapercut.com

Penny Black Inc.
(800) 488-3669
www.pennyblackinc.com

Pink Paislee
(816) 883-8259
www.pinkpaislee.com

Plaid Enterprises Inc./All Night Media
(800) 842-4197
www.plaidonline.com

Ranger Industries Inc.
(732) 389-3535
www.rangerink.com

Sakura of America
www.sakuraofamerica.com

Scor-Pal Products
(877) 629-9908
www.scor-pal.com

SCRAPBOOK ADHESIVES BY 3L™
www.scrapbook-adhesives.
com

Scrapbook Customs
www.scrapbookcustoms.com

Spellbinders™ Paper Arts
(888) 547-0400
www.spellbinderspaperarts.
com

Stampin' Up!
(800) STAMP UP (782-6787)
www.stampinup.com

Technique Tuesday
(503) 644-4073
www.techniquetuesday.com

Tombow USA
www.tombowusa.com

Tsukineko LLC
(425) 883-7733
www.tsukineko.com

Waltzingmouse Stamps
www.waltzingmousestamps.
com

Want2Scrap
www.want2scrap.com
(260) 740-2976

Wilton Industries
(800) 794-5866
www.wilton.com

WorldWin Papers
(888) 843-6455
www.worldwinpapers.com

The Buyer's Guide listings are provided as a service to our readers and should not be considered an endorsement from this publication.